P9-DII-692

THE ZONE OF EMERGENCE

URBAN STUDIES SERIES

General Editor: George S. Sternlieb

The Affluent Suburb: Princeton by George S. Sternlieb, Robert William Burchell and Lynne Beyer Sagalyn

The Zone of Emergence: A Case Study of Plainfield, New Jersey by George S. Sternlieb and W. Patrick Beaton

The Ecology of Welfare: Housing and Welfare in New York City by George S. Sternlieb and Bernard P. Indik.

Landlords and Tenants: A Complete Guide to the Residential Rental Relationship by Jerome G. Rose.

Young Families in Transition: A Social Psychological Study by Ludwig L. Geismar.

HD4606
P56
574

THE ZONE
OF EMERGENCE

A CASE STUDY
OF PLAINFIELD, NEW JERSEY

GEORGE STERNLIEB
W. PATRICK BEATON

ta

Transaction Books
New Brunswick, New Jersey
Distributed by E.P. Dutton & Company

MAY 3 1974

182085

Copyright © 1972 by Transaction, Inc.
New Brunswick, New Jersey

All rights reserved. No part of this publication may be reproduced or transmitted in any
form or by any means, electronic or mechanical, including photocopy, recording or any
information storage and retrieval system, without prior permission in writing
from the publisher.

Printed in the United States of America
Library of Congress Catalog Number: 78-186710
ISBN: 0-87855-035-6

This volume was prepared for the
city of Plainfield, New Jersey
by the
Center for Urban Policy Research
Rutgers The State University
New Brunswick, New Jersey

"It is hoped that these pages will show that from an economic, a political, and a cultural point of view, the districts immediately between the old city and the suburbs constitute a single sociological fact with a sharply defined significance and appeal."

> Robert A. Woods, referring to the old inner suburbs ringing the city's core *(The Zone of Emergence,* circa 1910-1920, Harvard University Press, 1962).

CONTENTS

LIST OF EXHIBITS

ACKNOWLEDGEMENTS

This is a study of a complex phenomenon—a city as a service delivery system. The variety of elements—education, police, fire, welfare, hospital and so on—that must be considered here is evident. Our efforts required the ingenuity and cooperation of an equally diverse group of individuals. To single out a few is to do less than justice to many.

With this broader group in mind, the authors must acknowledge the contribution of Mrs. Mildred Barry, whose critical commentaries and creative support were essential to the study. Mrs. Gloria Adlerman, Mr. Michael Miernik, Mr. James Alexander, Mr. Kenneth Lipner and Mr. Robert Abramson were responsible for much of the field work upon which our observations are based. Mrs. Mary Wenz and Mrs. Alice Mallory did yeoman work in the field. In addition, the editorial inputs of Professor Susan Fainstein were substantial.

The text pages were produced and checked by Mrs. Mary Picarella, Mr. Dominic Salluce and Mrs. Mary Gillies. Editing was done by Mrs. Gloria R. Cook. We are grateful for their tireless reminders and corrections.

This study would have been impossible without the active and positive support secured from every member of the official governmental Plainfield family. The goodwill and cooperation which was received from every level of the municipality is a tribute to the belief and hopes in the future of the community by its government. Mayor Frank H. Blatz, Jr., City Administrator Kennedy Shaw, Director of Administration Daniel P. Kiely, Jr., Superintendent of Schools Russell W.

Carpenter, Jr., and Director of Public Affairs and Safety Charles Allen extended continuing support.

In addition, the individual department heads and their staffs generously gave time to explain, criticize and amplify our work. Much of whatever virtue this study may possess comes from the contributions of Lieutenant Leo T. Wilson of the Police Division, Chief John Townley of the Fire Division, Mr. Bayard M. Manser of the Office of Finance, Mr. Lynniel Moore of the Public Library, Mr. John F. Kunze, the Health Officer, Mr. Francis Sabino of the Recreation Department and Mr. Elliot Weinstein of the Planning Department.

We are especially grateful to Mrs. Ruth H. Dudley and the staff of the Welfare Department for their insights regarding Plainfield's human problems and population shifts within the recent past.

This is a working document. Its merits are largely a tribute to its outside contributors; its demerits are the authors' own. It is our hope that it will provide a framework for creative action.

INTRODUCTION

The drama and turbulence of major cities' core areas, and the tragedy of violence and the misery of conditions which have generated it have dominated both the headlines and the thinking of academicians and government officials. Unnoted has been the development of "zones of emergence"—older suburbs which are open to minority group émigrés from core cities. Typically, these zones have reasonably substantial housing available at relatively low prices. They are increasingly becoming staging grounds for the upwardly mobile blacks and Puerto Ricans who are following in the footsteps of earlier groups on the way toward a middle-class orientation and setting.

Such an area is Plainfield, New Jersey—a community which serves as a safety valve for core ghetto areas. Areas such as Plainfield provide a target and a prize in return for following the conventional paths of work and saving. Increasingly, minority group members in the North are pursuing this prize. One of the basic questions of our time, however, is whether the goal will be worth the effort; whether Plainfield and other areas similar to it in function can continue to provide the infrastructure of schools, police and all the other elements which the émigré anticipates at the conclusion of his often difficult escape from the larger city's core.

The term *zone of emergence* was first used by Robert Wood at the turn of the century to describe the peripheral areas of Boston: the "trolley car suburbs" which were the locus of the second and third moves outward of the older ethnic minority groups who had originally lived in the hard-core slums of Boston. What East Cambridge and

1

Somerville were to the dockside areas of Boston at the turn of the century, the Plainfields of America are to the Central Wards of Newark, the Brownsvilles of New York City, the Hough areas of Cleveland and their equivalents. They give evidence that areas of housing, of a reasonable style and physical format of life, are open to minority group members at costs that the more successful of them can hope to afford.

Can these areas provide services to the newcomers? The answer to this question is not so much subject to the vagaries of will as to the fiscal dilemma. As will be shown later in this study, the costs of providing essential municipal services are soaring and new considerations (such as public health patterns, ecology and water pollution) are engendering many new activities, causing further pressure on the city's fiscal system. The fiscal capacity of the older suburbs is particularly sensitive to their changing economic functions.

The city of 46,862 people which will be examined in detail in the body of this document is located in New Jersey, a state famous for its low level of support to municipalities, causing their dependence upon local resources (typically the property tax) for the bulk of local community wherewithal. New Jersey's level of support only accentuates the problems described in this study; it does not, however, differentiate Plainfield significantly from similar areas.

At about the turn of the century the development of the suburban trolley car lines produced an outward shift in segments of the central city population. To a certain degree these early emigre shifts in residence were accompanied by commerce and industry. Lack of refrigeration and transportation limitations meant that most products were retailed close to where they were produced. Similarly, industrial intensification frequently followed on the heels of the worker émigrés. This is no longer the case.

Now, highways, rather than core-oriented mass transit facilities, provide the framework of business development, and the older suburb has often been overlooked as commerce and industry have grown. A city such as Plainfield was once the dominant retail locus within its region. Increasingly, however, this function has been usurped by the highway-oriented facilities outside the city's boundaries. Plainfield was, classically, a commuter town dating back to the development of the Jersey Central Railroad. The city acquired a major Mack Truck assembly plant located on the railroad line and drew workers from outlying areas. The assembly plant, however, moved out more than six years ago. While Plainfield sits proximate to the great band of industrial development between New York and Philadelphia, the new highway network has provided a host of alternate locations for new job growth. The former Mack Truck works is re-occupied, but by low-paying operations in search of cheap labor and cheap sites. The potential for increased economic development within the municipality is not encouraging.

The tax base, therefore, of the city is relatively limited, while municipal costs are rising very sharply. Rising costs are essentially a composite of two factors. First, a very significant level of year-to-year increase in the cost of doing basically the same business, i.e., the cost of delivering a given quantity of municipal service is increasing much more sharply than is the overall cost of living. Second, Plainfield's newcomers require a far broader range of services than the people they replaced.

As will be noted in detail in later chapters, this is particularly true in education. The problem is not only the number of students, but the need for remedial education to make up for the sins of omission and commission that are the legacy of children whose early years were spent in central core schools.

Basically, this economic stress is not a function of race. It would exist even if only wage differentiation and age migration patterns were involved. Race, however, exacerbates the problem. It is not only the absolute level of service but peoples' attitudes toward those services that determine the level of consumer satisfaction. And the keystone of successful government is the cooperation of the electorate. Public confidence in many areas is severely affected by the differentiation in race between governmental authorities—typically white—and minority consumers.

At this writing it has been three years since Plainfield endured its first significant riots. To the uninformed observer, the problems of the city frequently seem to be a function of that eruption. This is not the case; it is rather that the older suburb is now facing the same loss of economic function as has been noted in the major urban centers. It is in this light that the basic problems of service delivery and limited resources must be comprehended. The imbalance between fiscal needs and resources detailed in this study is far from unique. National response has lagged in facing its reality. And time is running out.

This survey is an effort to detail the circumstances of one particular city at a particular moment in time. The limitations of case studies— the possibility of their being essentially anecdotes limited to a certain time, a particular cast of characters and a unique geographic locale—are all too familiar. They have frequently driven the researcher onto the rocks of broad, computerizable analyses of publicly produced data which, in turn, may yield statistically significant but sometimes not very insightful or functionally useful work.

This is a case study of a particular community. The authors suggest, however, that the problems and dilemmas posed here are relevant to an understanding of many other communities in similar circumstances.

Before analysis is undertaken of the fiscal variables, it is essential that the reader have some feeling for the realities and attitudes of Plainfield's people. For this reason, the first chapter includes a description of Plainfield's residents, their attitudes and their housing.

Chapter I

THE PEOPLE IN THE ZONE OF EMERGENCE: THEIR HOUSING AND ATTITUDES

It is not only the absolute levels of services, i.e., the number of policemen, the speed with which the fire department can answer a call, the quality of instruction in the public schools, but rather the way these services are perceived by their consumers, the residents of the city, which is crucial to a municipality's viability.

Three probes are used to illuminate the attitudes of Plainfieldites in this section of the report: the first of them is a broad-scale study of Plainfield's present residents; the second, a look at home buyers in the past calendar year; and the third, an examination of a group of renters in a new apartment house. The goal was to answer questions such as: What are the attitudes of Plainfield residents toward the services provided by the city? Are there variations in these elements when newcomers versus long-term residents of the city are compared? Are there significant variations as a function of race? Who are the newcomers to the community and how do they view it?

These are crucial questions for cities such as Plainfield. The effort described here was both to define the population and to provide insight into its character in terms of variants of race and length of residence in Plainfield.

The three sections basic to this part of the study are:

1. Plainfield's Present Residents
   The results of 441 interviews secured from a telephone survey of all the Plainfield residents listed in the telephone directory as of April 1970.

EXHIBIT I-1

LENGTH OF RESIDENCE IN PLAINFIELD
(BY OWNER/RENTER STATUS)

LENGTH OF RESIDENCE	STATUS								
	Own		Rent		Other		NA/DK		Total	
	No.	%	No.	%	No.	%	No.	%	No.	%
1 year or less	10	3.9	17	9.9	1	16.7	0	0.0	28	6.4
1 to 3 years	28	10.9	31	18.1	0	0.0	1	33.3	60	13.7
3+ to 6 years	20	7.8	19	11.1	0	0.0	0	0.0	39	8.9
6+ to 10 years	33	12.8	22	12.9	1	16.7	0	0.0	56	12.8
10+ to 20 years	44	17.1	24	14.0	0	0.0	0	0.0	68	15.6
Over 20 years	79	30.7	30	17.5	4	66.7	2	66.7	115	26.3
Born in Plainfield	42	16.3	27	15.8	0	0.0	0	0.0	69	15.8
NA/DK	1	0.4	1	0.6	0	0.0	0	0.0	2	0.5
Total	257	100.0	171	100.0	6	100.0	3	100.0	437	100.0

Source: Telephone Survey.

2. The Recent Home Buyer
   An analysis of 51 persons who bought homes in Plainfield during the course of 1969.

3. The Relatively Affluent Apartment Renter
   A door-to-door survey of 41 residents of a recently built high-rent apartment house in the city.

(The methodology for each of these surveys follows the results.)

PLAINFIELD'S PRESENT RESIDENTS

The following analysis of the telephone survey is divided into three major sections. The first concerns the origin of Plainfield residents, then length of residence within the community and their reasons for living there. The second centers on attitudes toward community services, and the third focuses on the socioeconomic characteristics of the residents. While the basic analysis is along demographic lines, where there are salient data on owners versus renters or by length of residence in the city, revealed in the course of the tabulation, these are introduced.

LENGTH OF RESIDENCE IN PLAINFIELD

As Exhibit I-1 indicates, there is, as would be expected, a far higher level of turnover among renters than among owners. Twenty-eight percent of the former, as opposed to barely half that of the latter, have lived in Plainfield three years or less. Conversely, nearly half of the owners were born in Plainfield or have spent over 20 years there, as contrasted with approximately one-third of the renters. It should be noted, however, that roughly the same proportion, one out of six for each group, were born in Plainfield The provision of rental facilities, therefore, is more than simply providing amenities for transients.

REASONS FOR MOVING TO PLAINFIELD

If employment and "following my husband's job" are grouped, they make up the single largest response among whites to this question, nearly 30 percent.[1] This contrasts with 13 percent of the nonwhites who gave this response. For this group the single largest response came from the 21 percent who said simply that they already had friends in the community. An additional one out of six of the nonwhite respondents indicated that they had come to Plainfield because of its housing.

The other responses covered a wide variety of reasons. One, for example, which came from several respondents, was: "When coming back from the South, we passed through and we just stayed." Another, which was repeated with a similar frequency, was: "It was getting too

EXHIBIT I-2

REASON FOR MOVING TO PLAINFIELD
(BY ETHNICITY)

REASON FOR MOVING	White		Black		NA/DK		Total*	
	No.	%	No.	%	No.	%	No.	%
Employment	69	20.8	4	5.1	4	30.8	80	18.5
Better schools	5	1.5	2	2.5	0	0.0	7	1.6
Husband's job	28	8.5	6	7.6	0	0.0	34	7.9
Housing	46	13.9	13	16.5	1	7.7	60	13.9
Married	29	8.8	1	1.3	2	15.4	33	7.6
Family in Plainfield	53	16.0	17	21.5	2	15.4	73	16.9
Born in Plainfield	51	15.4	11	13.9	2	15.4	64	14.8
Other	33	10.0	16	20.3	0	0.0	51	11.8
NA/DK	17	5.1	9	11.4	2	15.4	30	6.9
Total	331	100.0	79	100.0	13	100.0	432	100.0

RACE

Source: Telephone Survey.
*Nine cases were excluded from total due to insignificance of the information.

rough where we lived, so we moved here." In general, there was a frequently voiced feeling of both whites and blacks that Plainfield was a nice city away from the mass urbanization of the big towns (Exhibit I-2).

When the owner-renter dichotomy is considered, employment opportunity is singled out by more than one out of five of the renters as compared with one out of six of the owners. Housing is the single biggest reason for the latter, with nearly one out of five giving this as the reason for their settling in Plainfield as against one out of 10 of the renters.

When the focus is turned to the 88 respondents who moved into the community within the past three years, out of 433 for whom there are longevity-in-Plainfield data, there is some degree of variation. In the recent emigre group, employment bulks even more formidable, with 41 percent of them indicating employment or following husband's job as the key factor. This contrasts with the longer-term residents, more of whom are in the community largely because they were either born or raised there, have friends and family there and the like. It should be noted, as will be discussed later in more detail, that employment opportunity as used here need not be located in the immediate area of Plainfield. Residents indicate a broad radius of employment location in northern New Jersey.

PREVIOUS LOCATION OF RESIDENTS

About two out of every six of the present occupants of Plainfield moved there from areas in northern New Jersey other than Newark. An additional one out of six moved from New York City. Newark alone was responsible for only 4 percent, with a wide range of other origins shown.

As Exhibit I-3 illustrates, there is significant variation as a function of ethnicity. The proportion of nonwhites coming from New York City is half that of whites. Conversely, the southern states were the place of origin for less than 3 percent of the whites, while they accounted for over 20 percent of the nonwhites. Newark accounted for 3 percent of the whites, while 10 percent of the nonwhites came from this locale.

When the same responses are examined for owner-renter proportions, there are significant variations. A greater proportion of owners than renters came from New York; 17 percent and 12 percent, respectively. Similarly, northern New Jersey outside of Newark accounted for 38 percent of the owners, in contrast to less than 30 percent of the renters. On reinspection these were mostly second-generation Plainfieldites.

One-quarter of the 88 respondents who have lived in Plainfield for three years or less came from New York City, a much higher number than is the case for the city's population as a whole. By contrast for the

EXHIBIT I-3

PREVIOUS RESIDENCE
(BY ETHNICITY)

RACE

PREVIOUS RESIDENCE	White		Black		NA/DK		Total*	
	No.	%	No.	%	No.	%	No.	%
New York City	55	16.6	7	8.9	2	15.4	67	15.5
South Jersey	13	3.9	1	1.3	2	15.4	16	3.7
South (North Carolina, South Carolina, etc.)	9	2.7	16	20.3	0	0.0	26	6.0
North Jersey (other than Newark)	121	36.6	22	27.8	4	30.8	148	34.3
Newark	10	3.0	8	10.1	0	0.0	18	4.2
Eastern states	34	10.3	9	11.4	0	0.0	45	10.4
Rest of U.S.A.	17	5.1	2	2.5	1	7.7	21	4.9
Out of U.S.A.	12	3.6	1	1.3	1	7.7	15	3.5
NA/DK	60	18.1	13	16.5	3	23.1	76	17.6
Total	331	100.0	79	100.0	13	100.0	432	100.0

Source: Telephone Survey.

*Nine cases were excluded from total due to insignificance of the information.

three- to 10-year category, New Yorkers represent only 14 percent. It is obvious, therefore, that Plainfield is sharing in the exodus from New York City. The potential of more migrants from this source is evident.

While only 6 percent came from Newark, more than one-third came from northern New Jersey outside of that city. (The north-south division of New Jersey is drawn roughly at the line of South Amboy.) With the exception of this data, however, there is relatively little variation among the several groups. Interestingly enough, the proportion of newcomers and long-term residents coming from the South has not altered markedly.

It is clear from these data that the southern states are not the major immediate origin of newcomers to Plainfield in general, nor even of its nonwhite population. Similarly, the Plainfield rental market is relatively broadly based in terms of the origin of present renters, with New York City playing an increasing but far from major role. The potential market will be examined in more detail in a later section of this chapter.

LOCATION OF EMPLOYMENT

As noted earlier, a significant proportion of Plainfield's long-term and newcomer population is there because of employment opportunity. However, this should not be equated with employment opportunities within the city's boundaries. Situated as the community is, amidst a major road network with access to a limited but still-working commuter railroad, the range of work migration is substantial.

Exhibit I-4 shows that only one-third of Plainfield's residents work within a five-mile radius of the city. New York and Newark combine to account for approximately 10 percent of the work locales, while 26 percent of the respondents commute six or more miles to places other than New York or Newark.

When this finding is analyzed by length of residence in the community, there are some significant variations. The relative newcomers are more frequently long-range commuters than are residents who have been in the city longer. Indeed, Plainfield and the area within a five-mile radius is the location of employment for less than one-quarter of those residing in the city three years or less. The single largest segment is the 31 percent who work outside the five-mile radius but within a 10-mile circle. New York City accounts for 11 percent of the newcomers, double the proportion of the 10-year and over category.

As shown in Exhibit I-5, there is relatively little variation between Plainfield's black and white occupants. In any case, it is obvious that Plainfield's heads of household spread across a wide geographic area in their search for work. The city is a haven for people who, for the most

EXHIBIT I-4

LOCATION OF WORK
(BY LONGEVITY IN PLAINFIELD)

LOCATION OF WORK	LENGTH OF RESIDENCE IN PLAINFIELD							
	0 to 3 Years		3+ to 10 Years		10 Years and Over		Total	
	No.	%	No.	%	No.	%	No.	%
Plainfield	14	15.9	21	22.3	56	23.0	91	21.4
5-mile radius	7	8.0	13	13.8	23	9.4	43	10.1
6-10-mile radius	27	30.7	14	14.9	21	8.6	62	14.6
More than 10-mile radius (except Newark and New York City)	13	14.8	12	12.8	23	9.4	48	11.3
New York	10	11.4	8	8.5	14	5.7	32	7.5
Newark	3	3.4	2	2.1	5	2.0	10	2.3
NA/DK	14	15.9	24	25.5	102	41.8	140	32.9
Total	88	100.0	94	100.0	244	100.0	425	100.0

Source: Telephone Survey.

EXHIBIT I-5

LOCATION OF EMPLOYMENT
(BY ETHNICITY)

LOCATION OF EMPLOYMENT	RACE							
	White		Black		NA/DK		Total*	
	No.	%	No.	%	No.	%	No.	%
Plainfield	71	21.5	17	21.5	2	15.4	92	21.3
5-mile radius	34	10.3	8	10.1	1	7.7	44	10.2
6-10-mile radius	48	14.5	12	15.2	0	0.0	62	14.4
More than 10-mile radius (except Newark and New York City)	34	10.3	11	13.9	1	7.7	48	11.1
New York	25	7.6	5	6.3	1	7.7	32	7.4
Newark	9	2.7	0	0.0	0	0.0	10	2.3
NA/DK	110	33.2	26	32.9	8	61.5	144	33.3
Total	331	100.0	79	100.0	13	100.0	432	100.0

Source: Telephone Survey.
*Nine cases were excluded. These either represented other ethnic groups or were missing information.

EXHIBIT I-6

OWNER/RENTER STATUS
(BY ETHNICITY)

RACE	Own		Rent		STATUS Other		NA/DK		Total*	
	No.	%	No.	%	No.	%	No.	%	No.	%
White	203	61.3	123	37.2	3	0.9	2	0.6	331	100.0
Black	43	54.4	35	44.3	1	1.3	0	0.0	79	100.0
NA/DK	5	38.5	7	53.8	0	0.0	1	7.7	13	100.0
Total	251	59.3	165	39.0	4	0.9	3	0.8	423	100.0

Source: Telephone Survey.
*Nine cases were excluded from total due to insignificance of the information.

part, work outside of its environs. Because the Plainfield housing market can provide such a broad geographic band of employment opportunity, it has great potential for attracting many new commuting residents.

ATTITUDES TOWARD THE COMMUNITY AND ITS SERVICES

The following material presents some quantification of responses to questions about the degree to which Plainfield residents are satisfied with their housing accommodations and the municipal environment of their residences.

OWNER/RENTER STATUS

Sixty-one percent of the white respondents to this question as contrasted to 54 percent of the blacks own their own homes. When housing configuration is analyzed, 59 percent of the whites live in one-family houses as compared with 51 percent of the nonwhites. Twenty percent of the latter group live in two-family houses, while slightly less than half the whites were so housed. The larger developments were comparable in the ethnic distribution of their inhabitants. Notice that about 9 percent of the respondents indicated that their one-family homes were rented.

It is clear from Exhibit I-6 that the two major ethnic groups of the city are not quite as disparate in terms of housing tenure as is sometimes believed. While there is some indication that, as discussed in Appendix A on methodology, the level of nonwhite renters is perhaps underrepresented in the sample, the basic generalization, that a substantial proportion of Plainfield's black residents are homeowners, holds.

SATISFACTION WITH PRESENT HOUSING

As seen in Exhibit I-7, if the sample results as a whole are examined, there is a general level of satisfaction with housing accommodations. Fifty-six percent of the respondents indicate that they are very satisfied, with an additional 28 percent indicating that they are pretty satisfied. "Poor" and "very poor" responses are less than 8 percent of the total.

When analyzed by race, however, the situation is quite different. Fully 61 percent of the whites say that they are very satisfied with their present housing accommodations as compared with less than 40 percent of the blacks. While "pretty satisfied" got the same response from each, the "poor" or "very poor" responses were given by less than 5 percent of the whites but by over one-fifth of the nonwhites.

The same responses were analyzed in terms of homeowners versus

EXHIBIT I-7

SATISFACTION WITH PRESENT HOUSING
(BY ETHNICITY)

		RACE					
	White		Black		NA/DK		Total*
RESPONSE	No.	%	No.	%	No.	%	No.	%
Very	203	61.3	31	39.2	6	46.2	243	56.3
Pretty	92	27.8	21	26.6	7	53.8	123	28.5
Neutral	18	5.4	8	10.1	0	0.0	28	6.5
Poor	14	4.2	10	12.7	0	0.0	25	5.8
Very poor	2	0.6	7	8.9	0	0.0	9	2.1
NA/DK	2	0.6	2	2.5	0	0.0	4	0.9
Total	331	100.0	79	100.0	13	100.0	432	100.0

Source: Telephone Survey.

*Nine cases were excluded from total due to insignificance of the information.

renters. The former are generally more satisfied with their accommodations than the latter, with fully 90 percent of the homeowners giving a "satisfied" or "very satisfied" response, as contrasted with 75 percent of the renters.

Why the dissatisfaction? There is no great variation by ethnic composition in the reasons cited for housing problems. The one major variable is the size of accommodations, which is mentioned by one out of 12 of the white dissenters, but nearly double that proportion of the blacks. Again the potential for discontent from the latter group is evident based upon this problem.[2] In general the renter response followed the black point of view.

Analysis of the response in terms of length of residence in Plainfield reveals no variation. Most Plainfieldites are satisfied with their housing regardless of their tenure in the community. More newcomers complain that rents are too high than do long-term residents, but the absolute level is relatively trivial.

SATISFACTION WITH LIVING IN PLAINFIELD

In general the responses, listed in Exhibit I-8, to the question, "Has Plainfield met your expectations?" are quite positive regardless of ethnicity. For the group as a whole 46 percent answered in the affirmative. Slightly less than 20 percent answered in the negative. Note, however, the 11 percent who volunteered that while Plainfield once had met their expectations, it no longer did.

On analysis of the response by whites contrasted to that of blacks, while the positives are quite comparable, the negatives are not. More than one-quarter of the black respondents—27 percent—answered in the negative, in contrast with only 18 percent of the whites. This, however, may be accounted for by the higher proportion of whites—12 percent—who answered that Plainfield no longer met their expectations, as contrasted with half that for the blacks.

There is little variation in the owner-renter response on this score, with the exception of the 12 percent of the owners who said that the community once had met their expectations but did not anymore, compared with 9 percent of the renters who gave the same response.

There is little variation between the several groups on this score as a function of length of residence in the community. About 55 percent of the newcomers unequivocally answer yes, with less than half that fraction saying no; the balance is scattered through the other categories. The only variation of significance is in the response rate for those people who have lived in Plainfield for over 10 years. Here only 40 percent said that Plainfield met their expectations. Seventeen percent said that it

EXHIBIT I-8

RESPONSES TO THE QUESTION
"HAS PLAINFIELD MET YOUR EXPECTATIONS?"
(BY ETHNICITY)

RACE

RESPONSE	White		Black		NA/DK		Total*	
	No.	%	No.	%	No.	%	No.	%
Yes	151	45.6	38	48.1	9	69.2	200	46.3
No	60	18.1	21	26.6	0	0.0	85	19.7
Did, but not anymore	41	12.4	5	6.3	0	0.0	47	10.9
Did not have any	14	4.2	2	2.5	0	0.0	16	3.7
NA/DK	65	19.6	13	16.5	4	30.8	84	19.4
Total	331	100.0	79	100.0	13	100.0	432	100.0

Source: Telephone Survey.

*Nine cases were excluded from total due to insignificance of the information.

did not, while 16 percent said that it once did but that this was no longer the case.

There is obviously wide variation in the degree of satisfaction felt for the community by newcomers and by longer-term residents. When the reasons are tabulated, the range is so broad as to defy description. Few respondents from any of the groups mentioned the tax burden.

About 10 percent of the negatives, interestingly enough, reneged on their earlier responses and, when questioned in detail about their reasons for the initial negative, said basically they really did like Plainfield.

PLANS FOR LIVING IN PLAINFIELD FIVE YEARS FROM NOW

Slightly over 40 percent of the respondents answered that they think they will be living in Plainfield in 1975, while slightly more than one-quarter do not feel that they will be living in Plainfield at that time. An equivalent proportion answered simply that they didn't know. The variation between blacks and whites on this point is important. Twenty-seven percent of the whites anticipated that they would not be living in Plainfield in five years, compared to 23 percent of the nonwhites. While the size of the numbers involved in the response rate does not permit tight statistical significance tests, to the degree that this type of shift takes place, the potential for a continued racial shift exists (Exhibit I-9).

If owner-renter status is focused on, the answers are obviously skewed by the type of tenurial arrangement. Only one-third of the renters, as contrasted with half of the owners, answered that they thought they would be living in Plainfield five years from now (Exhibit I-10). Approximately one-third of the renters indicated a negative response, compared with less than one-quarter of the owners.

Again, to the extent that this is a portent of the future, the relative stability of homeowners as opposed to renters is shown. (Notice that the level of turnover among owners indicated by this response rate agrees with the homeowner computations which will be found in a later part of this chapter.)

A wide variety of responses was secured from respondents who were planning to move. They ranged from "My family is grown up and is no longer in Plainfield" to "I am only here until my husband finishes school." Some potential movers simply stated that they wanted to move further into the country. A number of responses, however, suggested that education problems were at the root of their discontent. While there was some reference to racial problems, they were far from dominant.

Interestingly, when the responses were differentiated by race, no

EXHIBIT I-9

PLANS FOR LIVING IN PLAINFIELD FIVE YEARS FROM NOW
(BY ETHNICITY)

RESPONSE	RACE							
	White		Black		NA/DK		Total*	
	No.	%	No.	%	No.	%	No.	%
Yes	142	42.9	37	46.8	5	38.5	188	43.5
No	91	27.5	18	22.8	3	23.1	116	26.9
Don't know	95	28.7	23	29.1	4	30.8	123	28.5
No answer	3	0.9	1	1.3	1	7.7	5	1.2
Total	331	100.0	79	100.0	13	100.0	432	100.0

Source: Telephone Survey.

*Nine cases were excluded from total due to insignificance of the information.

EXHIBIT I-10

PLANS FOR LIVING IN PLAINFIELD FIVE YEARS FROM NOW
(BY OWNER/RENTER STATUS)

RESPONSE	Own		Rent		NA/DK		Total*	
	No.	%	No.	%	No.	%	No.	%
Yes	127	49.4	57	33.3	2	66.7	186	43.2
No	59	23.0	56	32.7	0	0.0	115	26.7
Don't know	69	26.8	55	32.2	1	33.3	125	29.0
No answer	2	0.8	3	1.8	0	0.0	5	1.2
Total	257	100.0	171	100.0	3	100.0	431	100.0

Source: Telephone Survey.

*Ten cases were excluded from the total due to insufficient data.

EXHIBIT I-11

PLAINFIELD'S BIGGEST PROBLEM
(BY ETHNICITY)

PROBLEM	White		Black		NA/DK		Total*	
	No.	%	No.	%	No.	%	No.	%
Racial and community relations	108	32.7	10	12.7	1	7.7	119	28.1
Drugs, safety, and law and order	36	10.9	27	34.2	3	23.1	66	15.6
Taxes	49	14.8	3	3.8	2	15.4	54	12.8
Location of businesses and employment	4	1.2	0	0.0	0	0.0	4	1.0
Sanitation and transportation	7	2.1	2	2.5	0	0.0	9	2.1
Attracting industry	5	1.5	0	0.0	0	0.0	5	1.2
Schools	23	6.9	8	10.1	0	0.0	31	7.3
Welfare recipients	5	1.5	0	0.0	0	0.0	5	1.2
Recreation facilities	3	0.9	2	2.5	0	0.0	5	1.2
Housing	18	5.4	9	11.4	3	23.1	30	7.1
Two or more of the above	6	1.8	4	5.1	1	7.7	11	2.6
Other(s)	22	6.6	3	3.8	0	0.0	25	5.9
NA/DK	45	13.5	11	13.9	3	23.1	59	13.9
Total	331	100.0	79	100.0	13	100.0	423	100.0

RACE

Source: Telephone Survey.

*Nine cases were excluded from the total due to the insignificance of the information.

clearcut pattern emerged. The only shift, and again the numbers are relatively small, was in potential employment changes. This was mentioned by 8 percent of the potential movers among the whites and less than half that among the nonwhites.

A somewhat higher proportion of newcomers is planning to leave the city than are long-term residents. This, as will be detailed later, is related to their comparative youth and tenurial status. In any case, more than 40 percent of the people who have moved into Plainfield within the last three years had plans which would take them out of the city within the next five years. This is double the proportion of those who have resided in the city for 10 years or more.

Employment opportunities or shifts in employment opportunity represented 11 percent of the negatives among the newcomers. It should be noted that only 43 percent of the 88 persons in the sample who had lived in Plainfield three years or less were owners, as compared with nearly two-thirds of the more-than-ten-year residents.

PLAINFIELD'S BIGGEST PROBLEM

In Exhibit I-11 the variation in response by ethnicity is very evident. Nearly one-third of the whites referred to race and community relations as the dominant problem, compared to little more than 10 percent for the nonwhites.

Conversely the issues of drugs, safety and law and order elicited only 11 percent of the white responses, but over one-third of the nonwhites. Note that the law and order category here was specifically in terms of safety in the streets and the need for more policemen. Drugs were mentioned specifically by only 5 percent of the white population but by more than one-quarter of the nonwhites.

Newcomers feel most strongly that racial problems and internal community relationships are the largest problems facing the city. Nearly 60 percent of those people who had been in the city for three years or less gave this response in contrast to slightly over 42 percent of the longer-term residents.

Tax problems were cited by 15 percent of the whites but only 4 percent of the nonwhites. Again, this may be a function of length of residence in the city. To the long-term white owner who has seen the tax rate increase, this may be a much more painful dynamic factor than to the more recent comer to the city who has "bought-in" knowing the tax levels.

The frequency of references to taxes was in proportion to the longevity of the respondent in the city. Obviously, in part, this bears upon tenurial status with many of the more recent comers being renters who may not feel taxes quite so severely. Even if they are home buyers, in a

EXHIBIT I-12

FIVE-YEAR PROJECTION OF CHANGE IN PLAINFIELD'S BIGGEST PROBLEM

			PROJECTION							
	Better		Worse		Same			Total		
PROBLEM	No.	%	No.	%	No.	%		No.	%	
Racial and community relations	52	58.4	25	28.1	12	13.5		89	100.0	
Drugs, safety, law and order	26	44.8	27	46.6	5	8.6		58	100.0	
Schools	12	50.0	8	33.3	4	16.7		24	100.0	
Taxes	10	26.3	25	65.8	3	7.9		38	100.0	
Housing	9	45.0	8	40.0	3	15.0		20	100.0	
Location of business and employment attracting industry	4	50.0	1	12.5	3	37.5		8	100.0	
Sanitation and transportation	1	20.0	2	40.0	2	40.0		5	100.0	
Recreation facilities	1	20.0	3	60.0	1	20.0		5	100.0	
Welfare	0	0.0	2	100.0	0	0.0		2	100.0	
Total number	115		101		33			249		

Source: Telephone Survey.

Note: Responses do not include "no answers" or uncodable multiple responses.

sense the tax rate has been capitalized into the purchase price of their homes. In any case, taxes are felt more strongly by the oldtimers in the community.

Schools were cited as the principal problem of the city by 10 percent of the nonwhites and 7 percent of the whites. This may be attributed to the larger number of blacks who have children in the public schools.

Eleven percent of nonwhites indicate housing as a major problem versus half of that—5 percent— for the whites.

Note that the adequacy of schools was mentioned by a far smaller proportion of the newcomers than by longer-term residents. Many of the responses falling into the "other" category referred to national problems.

ANTICIPATION OF CHANGE IN THE PROBLEM
IN THE NEXT FIVE YEARS

Interestingly enough, the racial and community relations area, though accumulating the greatest number of responses as Plainfield's biggest single problem, also has the most positive anticipated projection. Fully 58 percent of the respondents guessed that it would improve during the next five-year period. This is the highest for any of the problem areas which were quantifiable. Twenty-eight percent of the respondents in this area thought it would get worse, with about 13 percent thinking it would be the same (Exhibit I-12).

The response to drugs, safety and law and order was less sanguine. The "better" responses were slightly outweighed by the "worse" at 45 percent and 47 percent, respectively. Schools got a comparatively positive rating, with 24 respondents indicating that they would get better and eight feeling that they would get worse. Taxes elicited the most negative response, with only 10 of the 38 respondents who indicated them as the primary problem expecting their alleviation, while 25 (66 percent) felt they would get worse.

The housing response was a standoff and, unfortunately, the other areas yielded results too small for any level of generalization.

In sum, while there is a considerable feeling that Plainfield faces very serious problems, this is substantially countered by a feeling that the future is hopeful.

There is little variation in response by race. Approximately 30 percent of blacks and whites envisioned their particular significant problem as getting better. The negatives were 26 percent for the latter group and 30 percent for the former, suggesting perhaps a somewhat more sober attitude on the part of the blacks. Eight percent of the whites in contrast to 13 percent of the blacks said that the problem would be the same, with 36 percent of the whites and 27 percent of the

EXHIBIT I-13

RATING OF MUNICIPAL SERVICES (BY ETHNICITY)

SERVICES

RATING Weighted Evaluation*	Public Schools		Police Dept.		Fire Dept.		Recreation Facilities		Sanitation/ Street Cleaning	
	White 3.12 No.	Black 3.03 No.	White 3.97 No.	Black 3.22 No.	White 4.13 No.	Black 3.75 No.	White 3.18 No.	Black 3.14 No.	White 3.45 No.	Black 2.81 No.
Very good	15	2	83	3	107	8	25	3	31	3
Good	79	23	176	32	162	44	89	26	175	27
Fair	182	32	57	27	60	26	150	31	55	15
Poor	43	19	10	13	1	1	55	17	53	20
Very poor	12	3	5	4	1	0	12	2	17	14
Total	331	79	331	79	331	79	331	79	331	79

PERCENT DISTRIBUTION

	%	%	%	%	%	%	%	%	%	%
Very good	4.5	2.5	25.1	3.8	32.3	10.1	7.6	3.8	9.4	3.8
Good	23.9	29.1	53.2	40.5	48.9	55.7	26.9	32.9	52.9	34.2
Fair	55.0	40.5	17.2	34.2	18.1	32.9	45.3	39.2	16.6	19.0
Poor	13.0	24.1	3.0	16.5	0.3	1.3	16.6	21.5	16.0	25.3
Very poor	3.6	3.8	1.5	5.1	0.3	0.0	3.6	2.5	5.1	17.7
Total	100.0	100.0	100.0	100.0	100.0	100.0	100.0	100.0	100.0	100.0

Source: Telephone Survey.

*Very good = 5, good = 4, fair = 3, poor = 2, very poor = 1.

blacks simply saying they did not know. Obviously ethnicity plays a relatively minor role in this particular response. In general, home-owners responded more positively than renters on this score, with 35 percent of the former and 22 percent of the latter saying "better." New-comers are more sanguine than long-term residents, with 36 percent of the former compared to 29 percent of the latter hopeful that the community's major problem would improve.

RATING OF MUNICIPAL SERVICES BY PLAINFIELDITES

The goal of this part of the study was not to evaluate services, which will be discussed in the body of this section on an absolute basis, but rather to get some feeling for their adequacy as perceived by Plain-field residents. It is the vision as well as the reality which determines the level of consumer satisfaction. How do Plainfield residents respond when asked to rate the major services delivered by the municipality?

To develop data on this point, the following question was asked: "There are many services Plainfield provides. How would you rate the following?" The sequence which followed listed public schools, police, fire department, recreation facilities, and sanitation and street clean-ing. The ratings which were utilized were very good, good, neutral, poor, very poor.

The findings which were secured are presented in Exhibit I-13, which gives the absolute and percentage responses that were received. In addition, weights were assigned the responses: "very good" secured a weight of 5; "good," 4; "fair," 3; "poor," 2; "very poor,"1. The weighted response is shown at the top of the exhibit both for whites and blacks, for each of the several functional areas.

As is shown in the exhibit, there is a wide variation in the ratings given to the several municipal services. Both among whites and blacks the fire department rated highest, with a weighted figure for the former of 4.13 and for the latter, 3.75. Note that for the sample as a whole, 77 percent gave a good or very good rating to the department. The nega-tives—i.e., "poor" or "very poor"—received barely 1 percent of the total responses. When owners and renters were cross-tabulated, both were obviously on the positive side, with the renters being somewhat more restrained in their enthusiasm.

For every category under discussion, blacks rated municipal services lower than whites. This may be a function of the reality of municipal services received, or may be a measure of black attitudes toward the city as a whole. This is most clearly delineated in the atti-tude towards sanitation and street cleaning facilities, with a rating of 3.45 by the whites as opposed to a rating of only 2.81 by blacks, making this the lowest rated of the five services.

Given the variation in income levels between the two groups, which will be discussed later, this rating may be a function of the comparative economic strain imposed on blacks by the city's system of private garbage pickup. The relatively positive overall response of 57 percent, who indicated good or very good service, cloaks a significant skew by ethnicity. Fully 43 percent of the nonwhite respondents gave poor or very poor ratings, compared to half that number of whites. There was no significant variation between owners and renters on this point.

Recreation Facilities

Recreation facilities were generally rated relatively poor. Approximately 35 percent of both whites and nonwhites rated them as good, with slightly more than 20 percent of each of the two groups rating them as poor or very poor. In absolute values, the comparability of the ethnic response is illustrated by a 3.18 rating by whites and a 3.14 by blacks. The basic pattern of renters being slightly less satisfied than nonrenters held true here also, but the variation was minor.

Public Schools

The public schools received the lowest rating by whites—an evaluation of 3.12. The equivalent figure for blacks was 3.03. Thus, the rating of public schools fell below that of police, fire and even recreation. Approximately 30 percent of each group rated the schools as good to very good. The ratings of "very poor" were comparable—less than 4 percent for each of the groups. "Poor," however, was signified by 13 percent of the whites but 24 percent of the nonwhites.

It is clear, therefore, that the public schools of the city on an absolute scale are rated lower by nonwhites than they are by whites. Whether this is a function of differentiation in treatment of students, of unfulfilled expectations or, perhaps, simply of more experience on the part of the nonwhites, more of whom have children in public schools, is an open question. Again, however, notice that the general vision of the world in absolute scales was more somber for nonwhite respondents regardless of category. Owners and renters are comparable on this point, with a slightly higher proportion of owners giving the schools a poor or very poor rating. The relative figures were 20 percent and 15 percent respectively.

Police

Ratings of police were much more positive overall than those for the schools. Seventy-one percent of the total sample gave either a very good or good rating. There is some skew by ethnicity, however, with 78 percent of the whites but barely 44 percent of the nonwhites on the positive side. The poor or very poor ratings were subscribed to by 4 percent of the whites and 22 percent of the nonwhites. The weighted ratings are 3.97 for the whites and 3.22 for the blacks. Only the fire department scored higher.

There is little variation between owners and renters, though the renters tend to be more negative. Ten percent of the renters gave a poor or very poor response in contrast to 5 percent of the owners.

Evaluation of Services by Newcomers to the Community

In general, those who had resided in the city up to three years were at least as positive as long-term residents toward municipal offerings. For example, only 12 percent of the newcomers felt that the public schools were either poor or very poor, compared with 20 percent of the longer-term residents of the community. If we compare only those with children under 18, this same conclusion prevails.

In evaluating the police, there is no considerable variation, but there are some indications of a slightly less positive feeling on the part of those in the community for three years or less. For example, 60 percent of the latter gave the police very good or good ratings, compared with 75 percent of the longer-term residents. Neither the fire department nor the recreation facilities ratings have any significant variation, and the same holds true for attitudes toward sanitation and street cleaning.

* * *

In general the data reveal that there is a relatively positive feeling toward each of the municipal services that were evaluated. While minority group attitudes in general were less positive than those held by white respondents, in no case did the negative approach the positive responses in number. Considering that this is a period in which law-enforcement agencies have been under considerable stress, the relatively consistent positive rating given the Plainfield police department is particularly noteworthy.

The schools did not receive quite the positive evaluation that one might expect, considering the very real efforts that are being made within them. Again, the poor rating may be a result of disappointed expectations and may not be an accurate reflection of the school's achievements.

Despite the generally positive attitudes toward municipal services, there are enough negative reactions to suggest that the community still must work to improve its image before the consumers. In part, the improvement can be made by increased expenditures. From where is the money to come?

EXHIBIT I-14

NUMBER OF CHILDREN IN HOUSEHOLD (BY ETHNICITY)

NUMBER OF CHILDREN	RACE						Total	
	White		Black		NA/DK			
	No.	%	No.	%	No.	%	No.	%
One	41	32.5	14	28.0	3	60.0	59	31.6
Two	38	30.2	10	20.0	1	20.0	50	26.7
Three	19	15.1	10	20.0	0	0.0	30	16.0
Four	15	11.9	6	12.0	0	0.0	24	12.8
Five	5	4.0	4	8.0	0	0.0	9	4.8
Six	5	4.0	3	6.0	0	0.0	8	4.3
Seven	1	0.8	0	0.0	0	0.0	1	0.5
Eight	1	0.8	1	2.0	0	0.0	2	1.1
NA/DK	1	0.8	2	4.0	1	20.0	4	2.1
Total households	126	100.0	50	100.0	5	100.0	187	100.0
Total number under 18	304		134		5		461	
Percent of total households with children under 18	38.1		63.9		38.5			

Source: Telephone Survey.
Note: "Child" is defined as any household member under 18 years old.

SOCIOECONOMIC CHARACTERISTICS OF
RESIDENTS AND THEIR IMPACT ON THE CITY

Many of what are identified as community problems created by a shift in the ethnic composition of the population are more often functions of the relationship of ethnicity to age and size of household. For example, as shown in Exhibit I-14, 38 percent of the white households but 64 percent of the nonwhite households have children under 18. As the elderly whites of the community are replaced by more youthful families—a substantial proportion of whom are nonwhite—the impact on the school load as well as other ancillary services will be striking.

But as shown in Exhibit I-15, the increasing youthfulness of the city's population is not merely a function of blacks replacing whites, but also holds true of the newcomer white households. Nearly 70 percent of all the heads of households who have resided in the community for less than three years are under 37. Barely 30 percent of people in Plainfield three to 10 years are under 37, while less than one in 10 of those who have been in Plainfield for 10 or more years are in this youthful childbearing range.

If we focus on the 88 respondents who have been in Plainfield for less than three years, we find that 58 percent have children under 18. The comparative youth of the newcomer group is further revealed by the fact that nearly one-quarter of this group expect their families to increase in size, as compared to barely 6 percent of the three- to 10-year veterans and half that proportion for those in the community for more than 10 years.

There is a considerable variation in total size of household when analyzed by ethnicity. Fully half of the whites are one- or two-person households, in comparison to less than 30 percent of the nonwhites. Conversely, when households with five or more members are considered, the equivalent is 16 percent and 35 percent (Exhibit I-16). It is clear, therefore, that Plainfield is attracting relatively young households. If, for example, we had chosen to confine our analysis to those residents who are 48 years old and over, barely 12 percent of the newcomers to the community would be in our sample. Or if we had confined the study to those who had lived in the community for 10 years or more, we would find that more than 70 percent of the group is 47 and over.

When age of head of household data are analyzed by ethnicity, it is clear that nonwhite heads of households in Plainfield are much younger than their white counterparts. Only 42 percent of the whites are under 48, compared to nearly two-thirds of the nonwhites. Conversely, one out of five of the whites are 68 or over as compared with about one-third of that, 8 percent, of the nonwhites (Exhibit I-17).

EXHIBIT I-15

AGE OF HEAD OF HOUSEHOLD
(BY LONGEVITY IN PLAINFIELD)

AGE	LENGTH OF RESIDENCE							
	0 to 3 Years		3+ to 10 Years		10 Years and Over		Total	
	No.	%	No.	%	No.	%	No.	%
19 to 25	17	19.3	5	5.3	5	2.0	27	6.3
26 to 36	43	48.9	24	25.5	15	6.1	82	19.2
37 to 47	15	17.0	36	38.3	41	16.8	92	21.6
48 to 57	5	5.7	8	8.5	50	20.5	63	14.8
58 to 67	3	3.4	12	12.8	59	24.2	74	17.4
68+ and over	3	3.4	6	6.4	62	25.4	71	16.7
NA/DK	2	2.3	3	3.2	12	4.9	17	4.0
Total	88	100.0	94	100.0	244	100.0	426	100.0

Source: Telephone Survey.

EXHIBIT I-16

NUMBER OF PEOPLE IN HOUSEHOLD (BY ETHNICITY)

NUMBER IN HOUSEHOLD	RACE						Total*	
	White		Black		NA/DK			
	No.	%	No.	%	No.	%	No.	%
One	52	15.7	5	6.5	0	0.0	57	13.2
Two	113	34.1	18	23.4	4	28.6	138	32.0
Three	61	18.4	17	22.1	3	21.4	82	19.0
Four	47	14.2	10	13.0	3	21.4	60	13.9
Five	26	7.9	12	15.6	0	0.0	38	8.8
Six	17	5.1	6	7.8	0	0.0	26	6.0
Seven	4	1.2	5	6.5	0	0.0	11	2.6
Eight or more	7	2.1	4	5.2	0	0.0	11	2.6
NA/DK	4	1.2	0	0.0	4	28.6	8	1.9
Total	331	100.0	77	100.0	14	100.0	431	100.0

Source: Telephone Survey.
*Ten cases were excluded from total due to insignificance of the information.

EXHIBIT I-17

AGE OF HEAD OF HOUSEHOLD
(BY ETHNICITY)

RACE

AGE	White		Black		NA/DK		Total*	
	No.	%	No.	%	No..	%	No.	%
19 to 25	19	5.7	7	8.9	1	7.7	27	6.3
26 to 36	58	17.5	22	27.8	0	0.0	83	19.2
37 to 47	63	19.0	24	30.4	1	7.7	92	21.3
48 to 57	45	13.6	14	17.7	3	23.1	64	14.8
58 to 67	68	20.5	5	6.3	1	7.7	74	17.1
68 and over	67	20.2	6	7.6	1	7.7	74	17.1
NA/DK	11	3.3	1	1.3	6	46.2	18	4.2
Total	331	100.0	79	100.0	13	100.0	432	100.0

Source: Telephone Survey.
*Nine cases were excluded from total due to insignificance of the information.

A later section on recent home buyers indicates that Plainfield's population will continue to become younger, as small families and families with post-public-school-aged children leave the city to be replaced by relatively youthful newcomers. The fiscal implications of such a trend are clear. (More data on this point will be discussed in the section on the recent home buyer.)

Education

There is an obvious imbalance between Plainfield's two major ethnic groups in terms of educational achievement. Three out of eight of the white respondents have had three or more years of college in contrast to barely half that number of nonwhites. Conversely, heads of households who have completed less than three years of high school comprise 14 percent of the whites, but 29 percent of the nonwhites (Exhibit I-18).

The owner-renter comparison is again useful; 38 percent of the owners but only 26 percent of the renters have three or more years of college (Exhibit I-19).

But while education levels do vary by ethnicity and type of tenure, their relationship to length of residency in the community is not so clearcut. In general, Plainfield's newcomer heads of households have much more education than their predecessors. Half of those in the community for three years or less have three or more years of college; this is true for barely 36 percent of the three- to 10-year residents, and only slightly more than one-quarter of those who have lived in Plainfield ten years or longer.

The undereducated—those with less than tenth-grade educations—number less than 10 percent of the newcomers, more than 15 percent of the intermediate group, and more than 20 percent of those who have lived more than 10 years in the community (Exhibit I-20).

Occupation of Head of Household

As Exhibit I-21 illustrates, whites in Plainfield tend to be employed in higher occupational categories than nonwhites. However, in absolute proportions, it is clear from the exhibit that Plainfield's blacks have a higher occupational status than those in cities such as Newark or, for that matter, the state as a whole. Fully 25 percent of Plainfield's black residents are in the professional/managerial category, for example.

It is reassuring to note, when occupations are analyzed by longevity in Plainfield, that newcomers tend to be in much higher occupational categories than longer-term residents. Nearly 50 percent of those who have moved into Plainfield during the last three years are in the professional or managerial category. This is true of one-third of the three-

EXHIBIT I-18

HIGHEST GRADE COMPLETED BY HEAD OF HOUSEHOLD (BY ETHNICITY)

HIGHEST GRADE COMPLETED	White		Black		RACE NA/DK		Total*	
	No.	%	No.	%	No.	%	No.	%
None	0	0.0	2	2.5	0	0.0	2	0.5
Up to 4th grade	6	1.8	4	5.1	1	7.7	11	2.5
5th to 8th grade	30	9.1	7	8.9	1	7.7	40	9.3
9th to 10th grade	12	3.6	10	12.7	1	7.7	23	5.3
11th to 12th grade	117	35.3	31	39.2	3	23.1	154	35.6
2 yrs. or less college	29	8.8	5	6.3	0	0.0	34	7.9
3 to 4 yrs. college	91	27.5	8	10.1	0	0.0	101	23.4
Above college level	33	10.0	7	8.9	1	7.7	42	9.7
NA/DK	13	3.9	5	6.3	6	46.2	25	5.8
Total	331	100.0	79	100.0	13	100.0	432	100.0

Source: Telephone Survey.

*Nine cases were excluded from total due to insignificance of the information.

EXHIBIT I-19

HIGHEST GRADE COMPLETED BY HEAD OF HOUSEHOLD (BY OWNER/RENTER STATUS)

HIGHEST GRADE COMPLETED	STATUS							
	Own		Rent		NA/DK		Total	
	No.	%	No.	%	No.	%	No.	%
None	1	0.4	1	0.6	0	0.0	2	0.5
Up to 4th grade	4	1.6	6	3.6	0	0.0	11	2.5
5th to 8th grade	22	8.6	17	10.1	0	0.0	40	9.3
9th to 10th grade	8	3.1	15	8.9	0	0.0	23	5.3
11th to 12th grade	92	36.1	60	35.5	1	33.3	154	35.6
2 years or less of college	17	6.7	17	10.1	0	0.0	34	7.9
3 to 4 years college	67	26.3	33	19.5	1	33.3	101	23.4
Above college level	30	11.8	11	6.5	0	0.0	42	9.7
NA/DK	14	5.5	9	5.3	1	33.3	25	5.8
Total	255	100.0	169	100.0	3	100.0	432	100.0

Source: Telephone Survey.

EXHIBIT I-20

HIGHEST GRADE COMPLETED BY HEAD OF HOUSEHOLD (BY LONGEVITY IN PLAINFIELD)

HIGHEST GRADE COMPLETED	LENGTH OF RESIDENCE							
	0 to 3 Years		3+ to 10 Years		10 Years and Over		Total	
	No.	%	No.	%	No.	%	No.	%
None	0	0.0	1	1.1	1	0.4	2	0.5
Up to 4th grade	2	2.3	1	1.1	8	3.3	11	2.6
5th to 8th grade	6	6.8	6	6.4	26	10.7	38	8.9
9th to 10th grade	0	0.0	7	7.4	15	6.1	22	5.2
11th to 12th grade	22	25.0	32	34.0	97	39.8	151	35.4
2 years or less college	10	11.4	7	7.4	17	7.0	34	8.0
3 to 4 years college	32	36.4	21	22.3	48	19.7	101	23.7
Above college level	12	13.6	13	13.8	17	7.0	42	9.9
NA/DK	4	4.5	6	6.4	15	6.1	25	5.9
Total	88	100.0	94	100.0	244	100.0	426	100.0

Source: Telephone Survey.

EXHIBIT I-21

OCCUPATION OF HEAD OF HOUSEHOLD
(BY ETHNICITY)

OCCUPATION	White No.	White %	Black No.	Black %	NA/DK No.	NA/DK %	Total* No.	Total* %
				RACE				
Professional, technical	80	24.2	13	16.5	0	0.0	95	22.0
Managers, officials, proprietors (except farm)	38	11.5	7	8.9	0	0.0	45	10.4
Clerical and kindred workers	30	9.1	5	6.3	1	7.7	39	9.0
Craftsmen, foremen, kindred workers	39	11.8	13	16.5	3	23.1	57	13.2
Household and service workers	37	11.2	14	17.7	0	0.0	52	12.0
Laborers (including farm)	12	3.6	10	12.7	0	0.0	23	5.3
Miscellaneous (students, retired, armed forces)	77	23.3	8	10.1	1	7.7	86	19.9
Unemployed	3	0.9	4	5.1	0	0.0	7	1.6
NA/DK	15	4.5	5	6.3	8	61.5	28	6.5
Total	331	100.0	79	100.0	13	100.0	432	100.0

Source: Telephone Survey.

*Nine cases were excluded from total due to insignificance of the information.

EXHIBIT I-22

OCCUPATION OF HEAD OF HOUSEHOLD (BY LONGEVITY IN PLAINFIELD)

OCCUPATION	LENGTH OF RESIDENCE							
	0 to 3 Years		3+ to 10 Years		10 Years and Over		Total	
	No.	%	No.	%	No.	%	No.	%
	31	35.2	21	22.3	43	17.6	95	22.3
Professional, technical	12	13.6	11	11.7	22	9.0	45	10.6
Managers, officials, proprietors (except farm)	10	11.4	7	7.4	22	9.0	39	9.2
Clerical and kindred worker	15	17.0	14	14.9	27	11.1	56	13.1
Craftsmen, foremen, kindred workers	9	10.2	12	12.8	31	12.7	52	12.2
Household and service workers	2	2.3	13	13.8	7	2.9	22	5.2
Laborers (including farm)	6	6.8	9	9.6	68	27.9	83	19.5
Miscellaneous (students, retired, armed forces)	0	0.0	2	2.1	4	1.6	6	1.4
Unemployed	3	3.4	5	5.3	20	8.2	28	6.6
NA/DK								
Total	88	100.0	94	100.0	244	100.0	426	100.0

Source: Telephone Survey.

to 10-year Plainfield residents, and only slightly over one-quarter of the longer-term citizens (Exhibit I-22).

It is clear, therefore, that while a substantial ethnic shift may be taking place, at least in the last several years it has been accompanied by a significant upgrading of the occupational status of Plainfield's residents.

Total Family Income

There is no doubt that the occupational data mentioned above are paralleled by the income findings. Over 30 percent of the black respondents have incomes under $5,000 as compared with barely half that percentage of whites. It should be noted, however, that Plainfield has a significant number of middle- and upper-middle-income black families. More than one-quarter of the respondents of that ethnic group were in the $10,000 and above income group. While this figure is obviously lower than the equivalent 40 percent for whites, on an absolute base it implies something of the character of Plainfield's minority group residents.

However, when the income data are analyzed by length of residence in the community, the picture is more optimistic. It is clear from Exhibit I-23 that the income levels of newcomers to Plainfield are comparable to those of longer-term residents. Less than 5 percent of the 88 respondents who have been in the city for less than three years make less than $5,000 a year. The balance of the respondents are nearly evenly split between the $5,000 to $10,000 group and the $10,000 and over group. Subject to research limitations, this implies that the newcomers are comparable to longer-term residents.

* * *

Plainfield is a city of white and black residents. The black residents in general have higher occupational and income levels than is characteristic of blacks elsewhere in New Jersey. They are, however, significantly lower than those enjoyed by white residents of Plainfield. There is a substantial exodus of older families whose children are too old for the public schools, making way for more youthful families, typically with a high proportion of children under the age of 18. Therefore, educational load projections, based on the aging of the community, which seemed obvious in comparisons of the 1950 and 1960 censuses, are highly questionable today. There is some indication that the number of children of school age in the community will move upward at a significant rate. The pressures upon the school system will be severe.

Plainfield's newcomers, judging from the relatively small sample

EXHIBIT I-23

TOTAL ANNUAL FAMILY INCOME
(BY ETHNICITY)

		RACE						
	White		Black		NA/DK		Total*	
YEARLY INCOME	No.	%	No.	%	No.	%	No.	%
Under $5,000	53	16.0	25	31.6	3	23.1	82	19.0
$5,000 to $10,000	94	28.4	21	26.6	1	7.7	118	27.3
$10,000 to $15,000	77	23.3	10	12.7	0	0.0	93	21.5
Over $15,000	57	17.2	11	13.9	0	0.0	68	15.7
NA/DK	50	15.1	12	15.2	9	69.2	71	16.4
Total	331	100.0	79	100.0	13	100.0	432	100.0

Source: Telephone Survey.

*Nine cases were excluded from total due to insignificance of the information.

that we have of them, are younger than the longer-term residents and have more children of school age. In terms of occupation and income, however, they are at least comparable to the longer-term residents. The challenges to Plainfield, therefore, are no longer the problems of ethnic shift per se, but rather of increasing loads on municipal services.

THE RECENT HOME BUYER

There has been little analysis of current home buyers in the older suburb faced with racial admixtures. Is there a pattern, as some of the more hysterical observers would have it, of a community turning black wholesale? Are only minority group members interested in buying into communities which are noted as being "open"? Who are the home buyers and what changes in their composition are occurring?

These are very important questions, not only for Plainfield but increasingly for other older suburbs as they become zones of emergence.

In the following analysis of 51 persons who bought houses in the city during 1969, the focus will be on the origins of the newcomers, why they moved to Plainfield, their attitudes towards the city and basic family characteristics.[3]

WHY DID THEY BUY IN PLAINFIELD?

The 50 answers to the question of why newcomers bought homes in Plainfield cover a broad range. Twelve respondents referred to the virtues of the specific house which they found at a price which they could afford. An equal number said simply that Plainfield was a better location. Eight of the respondents referred to a change in employment which occasioned a move to the city. Another half dozen commented simply that they had always lived in Plainfield and that the home which they had bought was a good value. The balance of the responses were scattered. It should be noted, however, that three of the respondents (all white) specifically referred to Plainfield as a place which provided a mixed community which had positive appeal.

There is some indication that the realty values available in Plainfield are highly competitive with those in surrounding communities. Thirty-two of the 51 respondents stated that Plainfield was not their first choice, but that after searching in other communities they had settled upon it. The economic reasons behind this may well lie in the price of available housing. One-third of the units sold for between $20,000 and $25,000, with an additional quarter of the respondents mentioning prices under that level. Most of the remainder purchased homes at the $25,000 to $30,000 level. Compared to the price structures in surrounding communities, Plainfield's housing costs are relatively modest. However, even these prices involve substantial carrying charges. For example, nearly three-quarters of the respondents answered that monthly mortgage payments, including taxes, are over $200. Less than 10 percent make payments under $170.

ORIGINS OF NEW HOME BUYERS IN PLAINFIELD

One-third of the new home buyers were Plainfield residents before purchasing. An additional 30 percent came from neighboring municipalities. Twenty percent came from other New Jersey areas; 18 percent came from a state other than New Jersey; and two respondents came from outside the continental United States.

The typical home buyer in Plainfield moved from an apartment—two-thirds of the respondents. Twenty percent came from single-family houses and just 5 percent from larger structures. The balance of the respondents had been living with parents or relatives. As might be guessed from the latter group, only 20 percent, had been owners prior to this purchase.

ATTITUDES TOWARDS THE CITY

The recent home buyer holds a generally positive feeling towards the city's offerings. While earlier in the interview the respondents were asked why they bought houses in Plainfield, at a later stage they were asked simply why they had moved to Plainfield. The answers were basically similar. Employment played a large role, with one-third of the respondents mentioning it. An additional 22 percent named the availability of housing, while 16 percent indicated that family or friends already lived in Plainfield and they were joining them. Fourteen percent reported that they moved "to get away from the big city." The balaᐧ of the answers were scattered among a variety of responses.

When asked whether Plainfield had met their expectations, half the respondents said yes. Nearly 40 percent, however, said no, with the balance giving no classifiable answers.

Why were there negative responses? Unfortunately, many of the respondents found it difficult to verbalize their attitudes. Ten out of the 51 simply had general negative feelings towards the community. An additional five respondents said that taxes were too high, and the balance of the answers were scattered. In general, however, the negatives were in the minority. Three-fifths of the respondents indicated that they planned to be living in Plainfield five years from now. The balance were split between 25 percent who said no and 15 percent who simply did not know.

When residents were asked to evaluate the services which Plainfield provides, their responses were generally positive. Forty-six percent of the respondents, for example, rated public education as either good or very good, while only 28 percent said it was poor or very poor. The police department was positively evaluated by 72 percent, with only 10 percent giving poor or very poor responses. The fire department received an even higher number of positive evaluations, while recreation was rated positively by 56 percent, negatively by 26 percent. The poorest responses were given to sanitation and street cleaning. Here, only 42 percent gave a positive response as compared with 48 percent who were negative.

It is clear that, with the exception of sanitation, the attitudes of newcomers towards the amenities provided by the city are quite positive.

When asked what the biggest problem facing Plainfield was, the responses had a broad sweep. Twenty-four percent stated that taxes were too high. (It should be noted here that in response to another question, 66 percent of the new home buyers said their present housing accommodations represented a much greater expenditure than their prior residence.) Race was mentioned by an additional 20 percent, with drugs, community relations, and law and order each getting less than 5 percent. The schools were mentioned by 14 percent of the respondents. The balance of the answers were scattered.

In general, the new home buyers were not as sanguine as the total sample about the future. Only 19 out of the 51 felt that the situation in question would get better, while 20 felt that it would get worse. Four felt that it would not change, while eight simply said that they did not know.

Satisfaction With Housing

Nearly two-thirds of the sample (32 out of 51) reported that they were very satisfied with their present housing. An additional 22 percent said they were pretty satisfied. Only 6 percent gave an unsatisfactory or very unsatisfactory response. When these last answers were tabulated, interestingly enough, they were found to be the responses of black owners of multiple-family houses. Their typical complaints referred to the size and general condition of the house in question.

CHARACTERISTICS OF THE CURRENT HOME BUYER

The typical home buyer in Plainfield has a family of five (32 percent). There is an additional 14 percent of four-person households, and an equivalent percentage of six-person households. The number of smaller households is nearly equal to the larger households.

Plainfield's new home buyers are relatively young: 64 percent are under 36 years old, with an additional 32 percent between the ages of 36 and 49. Only three out of the 51 are 50 years old or more.

The 51 recent home buyers have 81 children attending Plainfield's public schools; in addition, 38 of the 51 respondents have preschool children. This probably is approximately the total school load to be anticipated from this group since in another context only 20 percent said they expected the size of their household to increase over the next five years. But the fiscal burden remains clear. As the older home-owners of Plainfield are replaced by younger people with children of public school age, an increase in spending on schooling must be expected.

Even accepting the present ratio of 1.6 students per household, given the current average per weighted pupil school cost of approximately $866, the total school bill per household would average nearly $1,400. If the present prorating of education costs to other costs is assumed, the average home newly purchased in Plainfield would have to support over $2,500 in tax revenue to pay its own way. Obviously, while these costs may be borne in part by nonresidential sources, certain property tax increases must be enacted.

In general, Plainfield's current home buyers are better educated than community residents as a whole. More than half have some college, while only 12 percent have less than an eleventh grade education. Similarly, their occupational level is higher than that of Plainfield as a whole, with slightly more than half (52 percent) in professional or managerial capacities and 10 percent at the clerical levels. Twenty-two percent are craftsmen, and the rest are equally divided between service and household occupations.

The Plainfield housing market, while strongly conditioned by employment opportunity, is far from dependent upon immediate employment location. Only 10 percent of the new owners work in Plainfield, with an additional 12 percent outside of Plainfield but within a five-mile radius. More than three-quarters, therefore, work outside this range, with fully one-third outside a ten-mile radius. Only 8 percent work in New York City. It is clear, therefore, as will be seen in more detail when new apartment dwellers are considered, that Plainfield as a housing location has wide appeal.

As might be surmised from the foregoing, the new home buyer in Plainfield tends to be significantly more affluent than the average Plainfieldite. Thirty percent have income levels of over $15,000, with an additional 40 percent at the $10,000 to $15,000 mark. Only 12 percent were under the $7,000 level.

Race

Half of the new home buyers are white, one out of the 51 is Puerto Rican, two are mixed marriages, and 23 are black. Obviously, the racial shift which is taking place in Plainfield is far from overwhelming.

Annual turnover rates based on this sample are approximately 8 percent. In order to determine the pace of racial change, it was important to establish the race of the prior owner of the parcel in question. If, for example, white owners purchased from whites and minority group owners from minority group members, there would not be any change in the total proportion of each group's holdings.

In the small sample for which there are data, none of the white owners had purchased from minority group members. Of the 21 minority group members who knew the previous owner's race, 17 were identified as white and only four as minority group.

The size of the sample is obviously inadequate to make definitive judgments; the implications are, however, that the proportion of total homes that are minority-group-owned is increasing on the order of 2 to 3 percent a year. Again, this proportion is not necessarily subject to straight-line extrapolation. As the reservoir of minority-group-owned homes increases, the pool of potential resales is increased, perhaps reducing the absorption of white-owned residences into minority-group ownership. Conversely, there is the question of a tipping point: what level of minority-group ownership will generate the widespread withdrawal of whites? Certainly, the level of turnover in Plainfield is relatively modest at present.

Is minority-group purchasing geographically concentrated within the community? At first glance a wide distribution of minority purchasers seemed evident. When, however, the blighted sections of the city are superimposed on the areas of minority-group purchase, a much more distinctive pattern emerges. The bulk of these purchases are immediately peripheral to the blighted sections of the city. The reverse is true for the white purchasers.

As Exhibit I-24 and its summary reveal, the variation in location is only partly explained by the relative distributions of prices paid for housing by the two groups. The tensions that can emerge in Plainfield as a function of this distribution need little amplification.

HIGHER PRICED APARTMENTS IN PLAINFIELD

The changing demographic balance of the United States, with an increased number of pre-childbearing households on the one hand and a larger number of elderly households on the other, has substantially increased the demand for apartment rental units.

Plainfield's residential development within walking distance of the train depot and the main retail business location consists primarily of relatively old private homes on large lots. Parcel sizes of half an acre, occupied by houses selling in the mid-$20,000 range, are not uncommon. The potential for apartment construction, therefore, is obvious. Land

EXHIBIT I-24 (SUMMARY)

LOCATION OF HOMES PURCHASED IN 1969
(BY ETHNICITY OF BUYER)

	RELATIONSHIP TO DETERIORATED AREAS															
PURCHASE PRICE	Inside				Peripheral				Outside				Total			
	White		Black		White		Black		White		Black		White		Black	
	No.	%	No.	%	No.	%	No.	%	No.	%	No.	%	No.	%	No.	%
Under $15,000	0	0.0	2	10.5	0	0.0	0	0.0	0	0.0	0	0.0	0	0.0	2	7.7
$15,000 to $20,000	1	16.7	6	31.6	1	50.0	1	25.0	2	11.8	0	0.0	4	16.0	7	26.9
$20,000 to $25,000	2	33.3	6	31.6	0	0.0	2	50.0	5	29.4	1	33.3	7	28.0	9	34.6
$25,000 to $30,000	2	33.3	3	15.8	1	50.0	1	25.0	6	35.3	1	33.3	9	36.0	5	19.2
Over $30,000	0	0.0	0	0.0	0	0.0	0	0.0	4	23.5	1	33.3	4	16.0	1	3.8
NA/DK	1	16.7	2	10.5	0	0.0	0	0.0	0	0.0	0	0.0	1	4.0	2	7.7
Total	6	100.0	19	100.0	2	100.0	4	100.0	17	100.0	3	100.0	25	100.0	26	100.0

Source: New Home Buyers Survey.

zoned for garden apartments in nearby suburbs, for example, is selling
at approximately $25,000 to $40,000 per acre, while areas open to high-
rise development can command much higher prices. Is there a market
for development of this kind within Plainfield?

In a previous study, *The Garden Apartment Development: A Municipal Cost Analysis*, it was shown that, depending upon configuration,
such rental units can provide a worthwhile ratable for the community.
Is this one path of future expansion for Plainfield?

In order to reduce some of the uncertainties that cloud the answer to
this question, a door-to-door survey was conducted in one of the more
recently built apartment developments in the community. This particular development was constructed within the last several years and has
units renting at $75 per room. There is a total of 54 units, all occupied
at the time of the interviews (late fall of 1970). Forty tenants were con-
tacted and interviewed. Who are these people? Do their shared characteristics give some insight into the potential of similar developments?

ORIGINS

The respondents split practically in half between people who have
been long-term Plainfield residents prior to construction of this development and those who were attracted from outside the city. The range
of the latter is very wide. Three of the 20 came from New York City;
southern New Jersey was the origin of an equivalent group, with a wide
scattering of origins outside of the state. Only a half dozen came from
northern New Jersey, excluding those who originated in Plainfield.

It is clear from these data that, in part, the new luxury building
represents a regrouping of the more affluent tenants of the city. In
equal measure, however, the city, despite its problems, has been able
to attract people from a broad area.

WHY DID THEY MOVE TO PLAINFIELD?

Employment opportunity is the single largest response to the question of why these residents moved to Plainfield, with 18 out of the 40
giving this as the reason. The only other substantial number of responses were those (eight out of the 40) who indicated simply that the
housing configuration was available in this particular locale. About 80
percent of the tenants are satisfied with their move, with the balance
either showing some level of dissatisfaction or simply having no answer
to the question.

Once again, employment as a reason for locating in Plainfield is far
from restricted to employment in Plainfield per se. Less than one-third
of the respondents work in Plainfield, with the balance scattered across

northern and middle New Jersey. One in five of the respondents works in New York.

When the total tenant group was asked whether they would be living in Plainfield five years from now, 40 percent indicated yes, 30 percent no, and 30 percent did not know. Obviously, this is not an inordinate level of transiency. The reasons for wanting to move are quite broad, with about 10 out of the 12 potential mover respondents indicating simply that they would prefer another area.

RATING OF COMMUNITY SERVICES

In general, this group rated community services higher than any of the other groups interviewed. The public schools, for example, only received a 10 percent poor or very poor rating. The strongest negatives were given to recreational facilities, with seven out of the 40 respondents rating them as poor or very poor.

When asked to identify the major problems of the city, seven respondents referred to racial and community relations, a half dozen referred to taxes, and the balance of the responses were scattered. The responses to the second question in this series, "Will the problem change for the better or worse?" in part reflected the group's transiency, with half indicating that they did not know. This response, on probing, as much as anything else was basically a "don't care." Those who did have opinions, however, in general were positive, with 12 saying that the major problem will be better, five that it will grow worse, and three that it will remain the same.

CHARACTERISTICS OF THE LUXURY RENTERS

Basically this group is older than the new home buyers. The ages spread across the board. Thirty-five percent are 58 years and over, with an equivalent percentage under the age of 37. The distribution is smooth across the age intervals used, with some skew toward the ends. The data indicate that this type of apartment dwelling attracts the elderly, perhaps tired of the management problems involved with a one-family house, as well as the relatively affluent new household.

Note that only one out of the 35 respondents for whom there are race data was a member of a minority group.

The education levels are quite high, with two-thirds of the group having had two or more years of college. As indicated by the education analysis, in terms of occupation, this is a relatively well-off group. Two-thirds are in professional and managerial occupations, while approximately 10 percent are retired. The balance of the occupations are spread across the board. Family incomes parallel this finding, with 80 percent over the $10,000 a year mark.

In sum, the potential for additional luxury apartment house development in Plainfield is not dependent upon job opportunities within the town itself. Occupants of such facilities, while attracted by employment opportunities around Plainfield, presently seem willing to travel 10 miles or more to their place of employment.

The generally positive attitude toward municipal services exhibited by these individuals may very well be a function of their household characteristics. In this light it should be noted that no less than 34 out of 40 (85 percent) had households with no people under the age of 18 in them. The half dozen households that did contain people under 18 had only one at most, typically under public-school age. Given the distribution of municipal expenditures in Plainfield, this survey clearly indicates that luxury apartment developments are both practicable from the viewpoint of renting them, and desirable from the viewpoint of fiscal balance of the area.

The very existence of a national housing shortage, combined with the limited amount of land zoned for multiple tenancy, perhaps gives the city a unique opportunity to engender multiple-family structure development. The land is available; the zoning is not a problem. Can the developers be found?

FOOTNOTES

1. The exhibit's percentages are worked out to one decimal place. The discussion, however, rounds the data to the nearest whole number.

2. The locational variable which may have a decided effect on the ethnic variation in response is discussed in the section on "The Recent Home Buyer."

3. For a description of the methodology used to isolate the new home buyers, see Appendix B.

Chapter II

ANALYSIS OF GOVERNMENTAL EXPENDITURES

The fiscal problems of cities faced with changing needs have been conceived of in varying ways. Basic to all the conceptualizations, however, was the implicit feeling that if one didn't examine the problems too closely they might go away. Typically, such problems were seen as temporary abnormalities—perhaps even as consequences of the organizational shortcomings of the city itself. Frequently espoused was the idea that the size of the fiscal pie and the virtues of the city were adequate. It was their distribution and the operational proceedings which accompanied them that were thought to be at fault.

As fiscal crises widened, however, these relatively comfortable views of the problem have dissipated. There is a basic incongruity between the needs of our society—particularly those given to the cities as their responsibility—and the capacities of the cities to meet them. The concept of revenue sharing which is slowly gaining momentum in one form or another is a reluctant tribute to the realization of this imbalance.

Plainfield makes available to us a much clearer vision of what the harsh realities are than is the case with larger cities. In the latter, all too frequently the clash of personalities and questions about the priorities of the governmental structure tend to obscure the basic message; and that, very simply, is that whole new approaches to the redistribution of wealth are needed in our society in order to serve increased public needs. The mandates, the requirements of service, have been specified and have generally been accepted; the wherewithal remains to be found.

The observations on expenditure patterns which follow suggest the comparatively minor role played by federal funding. In addition, the funds received from the federal government, either directly or indirectly, frequently involve additional expenditures from the municipality.

For example, the provisions of federal funds for capital improvements create the need for increased operating resources. Some of this can be traced directly. Much of it, however, is represented by the undercurrent of essential growth in staff and sophistication in the operations of municipal government. A Model Cities program, a Public Housing Authority, an Urban Renewal Authority, to mention a few of the federally funded operations, require that the municipality, almost in self-defense, increase its own staff to serve as liaison and coordinating agency for the multifarious new operations.

The rapid expansion in these activities has taken place in the face of a relatively limited pool of experienced officials and administrators. The consequence has been a severe inflation in costs and a thinning out of manpower resources. This problem is not unique to Plainfield; it afflicts other municipalities as well.

Plainfield's basic fiscal problems, moreover, do not stem from lack of capital so much as from operating resource limitations. The federal government is grudgingly beginning to recognize this. As yet the results are minimal. An exception, however, is the implementation of the Brooke Amendment which for the first time puts the federal government in the business of subsidizing the operating costs of public housing rather than merely supporting the capital costs.

There are few areas of our economy that have yielded so reluctantly to the possibilities of capital intensification and increasing the productivity of labor as has the service category. The amount of manpower required to turn out a bale of cotton is less than 10 percent of its equivalent a generation ago. In the last 10 years the number of man-hours involved in the production of a ton of steel has been reduced by more than 50 percent. The number of man-hours involved per hospital bed, per school student, have not decreased similarly. Perhaps they cannot.

In studying Plainfield, we had the advantage of studying a well-run, well-administered city. While any critic of municipal affairs can always find elements that can be improved, it must be said that Plainfield is a municipality which has had aggressive leadership and a strong mandate for improving its administration. There are, therefore, few problems of allocation or of political machinery to distract our attention; rather the basic fiscal realities become unavoidable. And these spell out a continuous pressure on the city as a result of the imbalance between needs and resources. Unless there are substantial efforts made to broaden the support level of the Plainfields of this nation, such cities will be overcome by the burgeoning needs they must attend to.

The analysis which follows first takes up broad expenditure patterns. From an overall point of view, where is the Plainfield dollar going? What is the balance between salaries and other expenditures? Where does the city stand in comparison with its neighbors of comparable size?

* * *

The following section will touch on some of the principle functions of municipal service and expenditure. These include police, fire, welfare, health, library and recreation departments as well as others. Attention will then be focused upon the single largest functioning area of the city, that of the schools and the board of education. What are the demographic realities which Plainfield faces? How are they being met by the schools, and what does this mean in terms of expenditures?

From the area of expenditures, the focus will then be turned to revenue sources. How adequate are they to meet the demands that are being spelled out? And, finally, as we project revenue and expenditures for the next five years, what is the balance which is anticipated?

Public attention and critics of the municipal endeavors on the social scene have concentrated their fire on the relative allocations of money. Should the board of health get more money, how adequate will be the provisions to schools—and what of the fire and police departments? Lost in this fight over allocation has been the basic picture of the fiscal balance of the municipality.

This does not yield easily. The reader is forewarned that much of the basic material which follows is as laborious in the reading as in the gathering. Despite this it should not be overlooked. We can no longer afford the romanticism implicit in viewing municipal fiscal service inadequacies as merely the results of poor management, as the results of those fellows in city hall or in the poverty office. No easy excuse will suffice. Rather, these inadequacies must be seen as part of an essential system of financing social needs which requires structural alteration.

MUNICIPAL GOVERNMENT EXPENDITURES

There are several ways of analyzing the expenditures of government. First, each department can be looked upon as implementing an integrated program consistent with legal goals. Then departments can be compared with one another and, through the use of past data, changes can be analyzed. Second, the generalized economic categories—goods and services—can be extracted from each department and their expenditures compared over the time period. This type of analysis will give the broad outline of the importance of personnel costs over supplies, but will need refinement to enable us to detect differences between inflationary factors and additional service levels. A third method is to compare expenditures in Plainfield with that of similar cities.

Each of these methods will be discussed; however, in this chapter only the broad picture inherent in the second and third methods will be developed.

PERSONNEL AND SUPPLY EXPENDITURES

Each municipal government expenditure can be classified as either for personnel or other items. Although this technique obscures the differences between individual departments and items, it permits an immediate focus upon the most significant class of expenditures and the determination of their rate of change over the time period of 1965 to 1970.

Corresponding to expenditure changes, there are changes in the value of money as measured by the Consumer Price Index (CPI). The CPI gives an indication of the relative price of a constant bundle of consumer goods and services corrected by region of the country. The use of this index will help determine how successful municipal employees have been in meeting present inflationary pressures, and how much of the change in expenditures for materials and services is due to inflation.

Exhibit II-1 shows the CPI for the New York-New Jersey metropolitan area and how it has changed over the time span for this study. It reflects the increasing costs for goods and services consumed by city government.

Exhibit II-2 shows the two broad categories of expenditures for city funds. Expenditures for salaries are consistently above 65 percent of the total municipal expenditure; at the same time, however, the percentage change in both categories measured on a year-to-year basis has

EXHIBIT II-1

THE CONSUMER PRICE INDEX
(BASED ON 1957 to 1959 = 100)

YEAR	CPI
1965	112.2
1966	115.3
1967	118.7
1968	123.6
1969	131.6
1970	141.6

Source: U.S. Department of Labor, Bureau of Labor Statistics, Consumer Price Index.
Note: Percentage changes were: 1965 to 1966 = 2.8%
1966 to 1967 = 2.9
1967 to 1968 = 4.1
1968 to 1969 = 6.5
1969 to 1970 = 7.6
Total percentage change from 1965 to 1970 is 26.2%.

EXHIBIT II-2

EXPENDITURES FOR PERSONNEL SERVICES AND MATERIAL

YEAR	Salaries & Wages	Annual Percent Change Salaries/Wages	Other Expenses	Annual Percent Change Other Expenses	Ratio of Salaries to Other Expenses	Salary as Percent of Total
1965	$2,348*		$1,072		2.3	69%
1966	2,446	4.2%	1,119	4.4%	2.2	68
1967	2,832	15.7	1,560	39.2	1.8	65
1968	3,143	11.3	1,454	-6.8	2.2	68
1969	3,500	11.4	1,499	3.1	2.3	70
1970 (est.)	4,280	22.3	1,993	33.2	2.2	68

Source: Financial Statement, City of Plainfield.
*Expenditure amounts are in thousands of dollars.

EXHIBIT II-3

PAYMENT TO MUNICIPAL EMPLOYEES

YEAR	(1) Average Number of Municipal Employees*	(2) Municipal Employees' Average Salary/Wage	(3) Percentage Change Average Salary/Wage	(4) Percentage Change in CPI
1965	377	$ 6,229	6.1%	2.8%
1966	370	6,611	19.6	2.9
1967	358	7,910	8.0	4.1
1968	368	8,541	7.0	6.5
1969	383	9,138	13.7	7.6
1970 (October)	412	10,388		

Sources: Blue Cross Insurance Rolls, Plainfield, New Jersey.
U. S. Department of Labor, Bureau of Labor Statistics, Consumer Price Index.
Plainfield Study, 1970.

*Based upon the number of employees both full and part-time who are on the major medical insurance plan. This excludes only those employees who have not or will not work for over four months on the municipal payroll.

been in all but one case consistently higher than the change in the CPI. Analysis of the effect of increasing the number of personnel must be undertaken so that changes due to inflationary factors and those due to greater service through more personnel can be distinguished.

Exhibit II-3 contains the average yearly number of employees on the municipal level and their pay. From this and the total salary data in Exhibit II-2, two other calculations are made: an average salary per employee and the year-to-year percentage change in this salary. The results of these calculations, columns 3 and 4 of Exhibit II-3, reveal that even with the correction for the increasing number of employees, larger per-capita salary demands are being met. Further, in all cases this percentage change in salary is greater than the change in the CPI.

Exhibit II-4 allows a comparison of the average municipal employee's salary with the average production worker's wage. As of 1965, there was only a $400 per year difference between these groups; however the municipal worker has been far more successful in increasing his salary than the production worker.

Expenditure for municipal employees is by far the most important aspect of the municipal budget. Over the last five years there has been an increase in the total number of employees and the relative cost per employee. When salary and wage levels are compared with the CPI and the salary increases of production workers, the municipal employee is shown to have bettered his economic position relative to both.

(It should be noted, however, that this wage-salary comparison with production workers is not a valid comparison of service and work potential. The calculations for the average municipal employee include upper and middle management, clerical and labor personnel, while the production worker category is far more homogeneous in terms of wages.)

COMPARISON OF EXPENDITURES FOR
SELECTED NEW JERSEY CITIES

The second type of expenditure analysis consists of a comparison of the growth of municipal expenditures for a set of New Jersey cities with a population similar to Plainfield's. Exhibit II-5 gives the expenditures for 10 municipal governments. It further permits a comparison of relative cost growth by showing the percentage change in each city's municipal expenditures from one year to the next, based on the previous year's total expenditures.

The extremes as shown in Exhibit II-5 are Irvington, which has increased expenditures 36 percent over the time period, and Hoboken, which has only a 9 percent increase. Plainfield is slightly above average over each time interval.

EXHIBIT II-4

**PAYMENT TO PRODUCTION WORKERS
IN THE NEWARK LABOR AREA**

YEAR	Weekly Earnings	Yearly Earnings	Percentage Change in Yearly Earnings	Percentage Change in CPI
1965 (August)	$111.52	$5,800		
1966	116.05	6,040	4.1%	2.8%
1967	119.84	6,250	3.5	2.9
1968	126.69	6,600	5.6	4.1
1969	130.87	6,750	2.3	6.5
1970	135.37	7,000	3.7	7.6

Source: New Jersey Employment and Labor Market, Division of Planning and Research, Department of Labor and Industry.
U. S. Department of Labor, Bureau of Labor Statistics, Consumer Price Index.

EXHIBIT II-5

MUNICIPAL EXPENDITURES OF SELECTED
NEW JERSEY CITIES

CITY	1965	Percentage Change 1965-66	1966	Percentage Change 1966-67	1967	Percentage Change 1967-68	1968
Bayonne	$11,665*	11.5%	$13,010	4.0%	$13,527	6.1%	$14,351
Bloomfield	8,711	7.3	9,345	8.4	10,132	8.6	11,000
Clifton	11,912	4.6	12,454	4.0	12,946	15.3	14,922
East Orange	13,325	9.5	14,593	13.8	16,613	7.9	17,930
Irvington	9,652	0.5	9,696	15.8	11,230	16.5	13,079
Hackensack	7,311	7.8	7,884	3.6	8,165	4.4	8,525
Hoboken	10,371	3.1	10,692	4.3	11,151	1.2	11,283
Montclair	9,119	3.4	9,425	6.2	10,013	6.1	10,626
New Brunswick	7,329	14.9	8,418	4.9	8,831	7.8	9,519
Plainfield	8,891	8.6	9,653	7.1	10,335	14.2	11,801
Average Change	- -	7.1	- -	7.2	- -	8.8	- -
Percentage Change of the Consumer Price Index		2.8		2.9		4.1	

Source: Municipal Yearbook, Table VII: Revenue, Expenditures, and Debt for Cities over 25,000, U. S. Department of Labor,
Bureau of Labor Statistics, Consumer Price Index.
*Expenditure amounts are in thousands of dollars.

EXHIBIT II-6

PER CAPITA MUNICIPAL EXPENDITURES IN
SELECTED NEW JERSEY CITIES

CITY	Population Estimate 1969	Percent Change 1960-1969	Dollar Value of Municipal Expenditures (per capita)			
			1965	1966	1967	1968
Bayonne	74,290	0.1%	$158	$176	$183	$193
Bloomfield	54,980	6.0	159	170	185	200
Clifton	86,500	5.4	138	145	149	173
East Orange	79,440	2.8	169	182	210	227
Irvington	64,130	8.0	150	150	175	203
Hackensack	36,620	20.0	199	215	223	234
Hoboken	46,160	-4.7	224	232	242	245
Montclair	44,630	3.5	204	211	225	238
New Brunswick	45,920	15.6	159	184	192	208
Plainfield	50,590	11.6	178	190	204	233
Average			174	186	199	216

Source: New Jersey Economic Review, Vol. XI, No. 6, Dept. of Conservation and Economic Development, 1969. Municipal Yearbook, Table VII: Revenue, Expenditures, and Debt for Cities over 25,000.

EXHIBIT II-7

QUARTILE RANKING OF KEY MANAGEMENT POSITIONS IN
PLAINFIELD COMPARED WITH OTHER NORTHEASTERN STATES

POSITION	Plainfield Compared with Cities of Population 25,000-50,000	Plainfield Compared with Cities of Population 50,000-100,000
City manager	3rd	2nd
City clerk	4th	4th
Finance director	4th	4th
Controller	4th	4th
City engineer	4th	4th
Director of public works	4th	4th
Fire chief	4th	3rd
Police chief	4th	4th
Planning director	3rd	2nd
Attorney	3rd	2nd
Director of recreation	4th	4th
Director of health	4th	4th

Source: Municipal Yearbook, 1970, Table VI, Salaries of Municipal Officials.

This comparison highlights the fact that all cities in the region have been facing greatly increased costs, and that the costs are not completely explained by inflation during the time period.

Does population size of the various municipalities affect their expenditures? Exhibit II-6 illustrates the per-capita expenditures for the same group of municipalities shown in Exhibit II-5. Both in dollar value expended per capita and its ranking within this list of cities, Plainfield is a little above average. This information also provides an explanation for the very slow rate of expenditure growth in Hackensack, Hoboken and Montclair shown in Exhibit II-5. These communities have had the highest expenditure level over the five-year period and, hence, their citizens apparently have not demanded higher levels of services. In the remaining seven cities, Plainfield included, citizens have demanded services which have not only increased expenditures, but closed the range from highest to lowest expenditures per capita from $86 in 1965 to $52 in 1968.

COMPARISON OF SALARY LEVELS
FOR KEY MANAGEMENT POSITIONS

This comparative study places the salary of key management positions in Plainfield's city government on a scale allowing comparison by geographic and population size. The geographic category used is the northeastern United States. Two separate population categories are used—municipalities below 50,000 population and municipalities 50,000 to 100,000 in population. The reason for including both sets of data is that Plainfield's population is too close to the 50,000 level to allow it to be associated completely with either group of cities.

The comparison scale being used is a quartile scale, which means that if Plainfield's position is within the first quartile, the particular salary is below at least 75 percent of the cases in northeastern United States; if it is within the second quartile the salary is below at least 50 percent of the area's salaries; and so on for the third and fourth quartile rankings.

Exhibit II-7 shows the quartile range for a selected set of management positions for areas of population above 50,000 and below 50,000.

* * *

To summarize the preceding comparative study, Plainfield has been consistently a little above average in its municipal expenditures, but in the last several years inflation, higher salary demands and increased services have pushed the expenditure rate higher than six other cities sampled.

Plainfield's changing expense pattern is far from unique. It is shared by many older, smaller cities of the nation. But the need and the demand for services continue unabated. In the following chapters of this study some of the major areas of expenditure are examined in detail. The growth dynamics and requirements described are clear, and the need for subsidization on a broader base is evident. Will national political realism be found to match?

Chapter III

ANALYSIS AND PROJECTIONS OF DEPARTMENTAL EXPENDITURES

The preceding chapter has presented an overall analysis of municipal revenue sources and expenditures. This chapter will focus in depth on specific divisions and departments of government in order to examine existing expenditures and project future expenditures through 1975.

Six departments have been selected for analysis on the basis of their absolute size and growth potential as well as their service importance. These departments are, in the order of their analysis, police, fire, welfare, health, library and recreation. To complete the analysis of municipal government, the remaining divisions are grouped within four categories: general government, the department of administration and finance, the department of public works and urban development, the department of public affairs and safety, and miscellaneous accounting categories.

POLICE DEPARTMENT

Next to the board of education, the police department is the most costly local governmental agency. To show the scope of the department and its high potential for increased expenditures, the various departmental divisions will be delineated and comparisons made between the actual as opposed to the authorized manpower strength. Following this, expenditure items will be analyzed, change mechanisms described, and the final projected expenditures through 1975 shown.

EXHIBIT III-1
DEPARTMENTAL SUBDIVISIONS, POLICE DIVISION

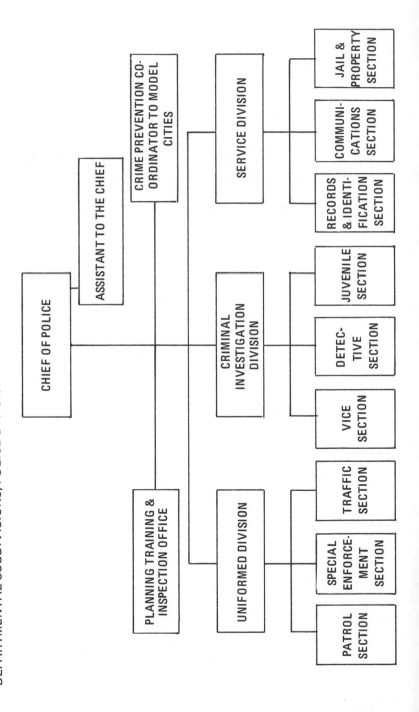

DEPARTMENTAL DIVISIONS

The department is divided into three divisions: uniformed, criminal investigation and service (Exhibit III-1).

The uniformed division performs those operations most visible to the public. It includes mobile and foot patrol operations within the city as well as a sizable civilian staff of school crossing guards. The criminal investigation division has three sections, specializing in specific areas: juvenile, vice and detective. The main functions of the service division are to keep the police station records, communications and the jail operating smoothly.

DEPARTMENTAL STAFFING

Exhibit III-2 shows the various staffing levels of the administrative and three operating units. The exhibit has been set up to show the

EXHIBIT III-2

**NUMBER OF POSITIONS IN THE POLICE DEPARTMENT
(ON OCTOBER 15, 1970)**

ORGANIZATIONAL UNIT	POSITIONS			
	Sworn		Civilian	
	Authorized	Vacant	Authorized	Vacant
Administration				
Chief of police	1	1		
Office help			4	0
Planning, training,				
and inspection office				
Lieutenants	1	0		
Sergeants	2	1		
Cadets	6	4		
Staff assistant				
to chief			1	0
Model cities coordinator				
Sergeants	1			
Uniformed division				
Division captain	1	0		
Patrol section				
Lieutenants	4	0		
Sergeants	8	0		
Patrolmen	64	8		
Special enforcement				
Sergeants	1	1		
Patrolmen	10	10		
Traffic section				
Lieutenants	1	0		
Sergeants	1	0		
Senior traffic maintenance manager			1	0
Senior traffic maintenance manager			1	0
Summer help			4	0
School crossing			47	8

EXHIBIT III-2 (Continued)

NUMBER OF POSITIONS IN THE
POLICE DEPARTMENT
(ON OCTOBER 15, 1970)

	POSITIONS			
ORGANIZATIONAL UNIT	Sworn		Civilian	
	Authorized	Vacant	Authorized	Vacant
Criminal investigation division				
Divisional captain	1	0		
Vice section				
Sergeants	1	0		
Patrolmen	4	1		
Office help			1	0
Detective section				
Lieutenants	1	0		
Sergeants	1	0		
Patrolmen	7	0		
Office help			2	0
Juvenile section				
Sergeants	1	0		
Patrolmen	4	1		
Office help			1	0
Service division				
Divisional captain	1	0		
Records of identification section				
Patrolmen	4	0		
Office help			6	2
Communications section				
Radio dispatchers			4	1
Jail and property section				
Patrolmen	4	0		
Matrons			1	0
Building maintenance			2	0
Garage maintenance			1	1
P. T. maintenance			1	0
Total	130	27	77	12

Source: Records, Plainfield Police Department.

likelihood of authorized staff increases; currently 25 new sworn personnel and 12 civilian personnel can be hired without a change in the municipal ordinance.

The greatest shortage is in the uniformed division, which is operating with only 71 of 90 authorized positions. Within the uniformed division, the patrol section has the greatest manpower shortage, with only 56 of 64 patrolman positions filled. The special enforcement section which came into existence in 1970 has not yet been staffed, adding 11 vacancies to the total. The criminal investigation division has two vacancies, one patrolman position in the vice section and one patrolman in the juvenile section.

Civilian manpower shortages, other than office personnel, include eight school crossing guards and one dispatcher.

PATTERNS OF MANPOWER CHANGE

The authorized size of the Plainfield Police Department has jumped from a total of 135 in 1965, to a proposed level of 207 in 1970. Interviews in the department indicate that this increase in manpower needs is the result of an increasing work load. Furthermore, changes in the crime reporting system have resulted in the unsubstantiated belief that there is a "crime wave." Prior to 1968, the reporting system was not complete. Under the new system, all police activities are logged. For example, calls requiring police car reconnaissance are assigned a number, and the time spent by the car on the call is recorded.

According to police records, the highest annual number of police calls and complaints had been 12,000 prior to 1968. In 1969, 27,000 calls and complaints were recorded. Crime has undoubtedly increased in Plainfield, as it has in most urban areas. The tremendous jump in calls, however, is probably more indicative of the change in the recording system than of a dramatic increase in crime.

The area of crime statistics is a highly controversial one. Perhaps a better indicator of the need for police personnel is the number of known criminal offenses. The FBI Uniform Crime Reports for Plainfield show that for the period 1966 to 1969 there was an 80 percent increase in such crimes. Exhibit III-3 illustrates these increases by year of occurrence and percentage change over the previous year.

EXHIBIT III-3

NUMBER OF OFFENSES IN PLAINFIELD
(1966 TO 1969)

	YEAR			
	1966	1967	1968	1969
Offenses reported or known to police	2,091	2,194	3,025	3,757
Percentage change over prior year	----	4.9%	37.8%	24.2%

Source: Monthly Count of Offenses Known to the Police, State of New Jersey, Department of Law and Public Safety.

If the increase in offenses was indeed 80 percent, the staff change throughout the years 1966 to 1969 barely allowed the department to keep up with the increased patrol, detection, and prosecution of this added load. Exhibit III-4 shows that the total police department staff has increased by 30 members—a 29 percent change from 1965.

EXHIBIT III-4

STRENGTH OF POLICE DEPARTMENT

| CATEGORY | YEAR | | | | | |
	1965	1966	1967	1968	1969	1970
Sworn	92	91	85	102	106	110
Civilian	10	10	11	12	15	26
Total	102	101	96	114	121	136

Source: Plainfield Police Department.

UNDERLYING CRIME CAUSES

Plainfield's police officials estimate that 30 to 50 percent of crimes against property are committed by narcotics addicts. Thefts of quickly salable items such as televisions, stereos and jewelry, in addition to purse snatching appear to characterize crimes of addicts.

The police are hopeful that a methadone clinic recently put into operation by Union County will be successful in alleviating the addict problem. Many police department members feel strongly that control of narcotics problems will produce a concomitant reduction in crime in the city of Plainfield.

Some department members, however, feel that the crime-narcotics link is not substantiated by police records. The record does not differentiate between those criminals who are and those who are not addicts. For instance, an addict arrested for larceny is recorded only under larceny, even if he is in possession of narcotics. It is therefore difficult to establish any significant link between the two.

Whatever the relative importance of narcotics to the crime rate, it is only part of the problem. Another contributor is the fact that Plainfield has the only housing stock in the immediate area available to low-income people, because of the zoning practices of the surrounding communities. This has resulted in a high concentration of impoverished minority-group members and the problems that usually accompany such a situation.

Plainfield's crime problem is, therefore, a function of the change in socioeconomic backgrounds of its citizenry as well as of the increasing use of narcotics. Thus, the police are limited in their effectiveness by socioeconomic factors over which they have no control. These factors are area-wide and must be treated at state and national levels. Otherwise, no matter what the police manpower or efficiency, they will only be fighting a holding action.

ANALYSIS OF EXPENDITURE LEVELS

Overall, police protection in Plainfield has increased 42 percent in cost from 1965 to 1970, with dollar values of $733,000 in 1965 and $1,764,000 in 1970.

The breakdown between personnel costs and other items is shown in Exhibit III-5. Wages and salaries consistently account for over 85 percent of the total cost and therefore are the crucial factor in predicting future outlays.

EXHIBIT III-5

POLICE DEPARTMENT SPENDING
(1965 TO 1970)

| | YEAR | | | | | |
	1965	1966	1967	1968	1969	1970
Salaries/wages	$667*	$710	$878	$1,033	$1,238	$1,563
Other	66	83	89	96	115	201
Total	$733	$793	$967	$1,129	$1,353	$1,764

Source: Financial Statements, City of Plainfield.
*Expenditure amounts are expressed in thousands of dollars.

In order to acquire some standard by which to judge police salaries and strength of force, six other northern New Jersey municipalities were selected for comparison (Exhibit III-6). Because the size of the police force is related to the population of the city, the table shows the ratio of sworn personnel to every thousand citizens. The range is from 1.7 men per thousand in Westfield to 2.6 men per thousand in Bayonne; Plainfield is the median value at 2.3 men per thousand citizens. With the increase in actual staff to 125 men, the personnel/population ratio will approach 2.5 men per thousand. It is not known whether the other cities plan similar increases.

EXHIBIT III-6

POLICE DEPARTMENT STATISTICS—1969

CITY	Population	Number of Sworn Personnel	Sworn Personnel per 1000 Population	Patrolmen's Salaries Minimum	Patrolmen's Salaries Maximum	Years from Minimum to Maximum
Bayonne	74,215	192	2.59	7,600	8,100	1
Orange	35,789	91	2.53	7,200	9,200	3
Perth Amboy	38,007	96	2.53	6,799	10,000	3
Plainfield	45,330	105	2.33	8,530	11,094	5
Rahway	27,699	62	2.21	7,698	8,988	3
South Plainfield	17,879	37	2.05	6,000	8,154	3
Westfield	31,447	53	1.71	8,725	10,000	5
Mean				7,507	9,362	

Source: A Survey of 1969 Salaries and Working Conditions of the Police Departments in the United States —
Fraternal Order of Police.
United States Census, 1960.

The salary levels of the Plainfield Police Department make it among the best paid of the group. Next to Westfield, it has the highest starting salary for patrolmen, while its maximum salary is highest of the cities shown in Exhibit III-6.

FUTURE NEEDS AND PROJECTED EXPENDITURES

Given the close relation between manpower and expenditures, a projection of manpower needs will enable us to approximate monetary needs. The force at present is short of authorized strength by 10 sworn and 5 civilian men. The filling of these positions depends upon the police chief's assessment of need. At present vacant positions are filled by the present staff performing overtime service.

In addition to increased manpower, the Policemen's Benevolent Association (PBA) will have a strong influence on future police expenditures. When the PBA goes into the 1972 bargaining sessions with the city, major contract items will be fringe benefits such as vacations, holidays and hospitalization. While present anticipation is that salaries may not be a major item except for cost-of-living increases, the potential for upward pressure is evident.

Because of overtime, patrolmen are often receiving more money than captains; consequently, more pay for officers may become an issue. The PBA may also demand a lowered retirement age, as it is becoming difficult for older policemen to function properly under present pressures. The number of years before maximum salary is reached will also be under fire.

On the basis of 1970 budget appropriations, and an increment factor of 10.6 percent (obtained by averaging the percent increases for the last four years of the average employee's salary) salary expenditures may reach $2,995,000 in 1975 (Exhibit III-7). This figure is significant as the large increment factor was derived during a period in which the number of personnel remained relatively stable. If, however, staff additions are required, this figure will obviously increase.

The projected expenditures displayed in Exhibit III-7 may appear high. They do not, however, include possible service additions. Moreover, in the light of recent salary demands placed upon other municipalities by strong patrolmen's organizations the potential for such a forecast is real.

FIRE DEPARTMENT

The fire division, which forms part of the newly organized department of public affairs safety, is the third highest expenditure item in the combined city government budget. Following education and police,

EXHIBIT III-7

PROJECTED POLICE DEPARTMENT EXPENDITURES

	Appropriations 1970	Percent Change	1971	1972	1973	1974	1975
Salaries/wages	$1,563	10.6%	$1,729	$1,912	$2,114	$2,338	$2,586
Other	201	15.2	232	267	309	355	409
Total projected expenditures	$1,764		$1,961	$2,179	$2,423	$2,693	$2,995

Source: See Exhibit III-5, p. 73.

Note: Expenditure amounts are expressed in thousands of dollars.

it accounted for close to $1,200,000 in 1969. Its growth is subject to both inflationary pressures and the increased work load.

EQUIPMENT

In order to reach all parts of the city within four minutes of alarm reception, the division maintains a headquarters and two fire stations. Major operations working out of the headquarters building include two engine companies, two ladder truck companies, the emergency squad and the communications center. One fire station each is also provided for the east and west ends of the city, these each maintain one engine company.

PERSONNEL

To give full protection throughout the week, four platoons of men, each working 42 hours, are required. The men rotate their shifts throughout the month.

Each platoon has a captain, five lieutenants and 18 privates. These men are distributed throughout the three stations, and are coordinated through the direction of their platoon commander. Each of the four platoon commanders is directly responsible to the fire chief.

OPERATING PROGRAMS

There are different programs in which various men of the division are involved. On the average, however, it is estimated that the professional fire fighter spends about 10 percent of his time on each of the following: actual fire fighting, inspection, training, maintenance of apparatus and hydrant maintenance; the other 50 percent is apportioned to standby time.

FIRE PATROL PROGRAM

This year a program to utilize more effectively the standby time of the men and equipment was authorized. This program (the fire patrol) maintains two to five cars with two men each on the streets from 2:00 PM to 2:00 AM. In addition to their traditional fire-related duties, this patrol is receiving police-oriented training for observing and reporting crime and related activities.

INSPECTION PROGRAM

The inspection program of the division involves visits and inspections of all businesses, public buildings and multifamily houses on an average of once a year. Inspection of one- and two-family homes is on a voluntary basis, however.

Partially as a result of these programs, but also because of the physical structure of the city, Plainfield has been given a Class B rating by the National Fire Protection Association. This ranks it among the top 14 of the nearly 600 municipalities in the state, of which only two are Class A.

EVALUATION OF PERFORMANCE

In the absence of accepted standards for fire departments, the best secondary means of evaluation is through comparison of Plainfield with cities in a similar situation. A set of cities, based upon population and location in New Jersey, was selected.

Exhibit III-8 shows that the potential protection given to Plainfield citizens, based upon the number of fire personnel, is midway between the extremes listed on the table; yet as shown in Exhibit III-9, with their new contract the firemen are higher paid than any department for which data are available. The absence of holidays and clothing allowances, however, may indicate possible new expenses to the city during future negotiation for benefits.

ANALYSIS OF EXPENDITURES

From 1965 to 1969 there was a large increase in the work load of the division. As column 1 of Exhibit III-10 shows, the total number of

EXHIBIT III-8

FIRE PROTECTION IN SELECTED
NEW JERSEY CITIES

| CITY | NUMBER OF FIRE DEPARTMENT PERSONNEL | | | |
	Total	Uniformed	Civilian	Firemen per 1,000 residents
Atlantic City	233	226	7	3.9
Bayonne	209	209	0	2.9
Orange	94	94	0	2.8
Hackensack	88	87	1	2.7
Plainfield	120	118	2	2.6
West New York	99	99	0	2.6
Irvington	153	150	3	2.6
East Orange	186	185	1	2.4
Bloomfield	118	118	0	2.2
Union	112	111	1	2.2
Passaic	109	107	2	2.0
Rahway	50	50	0	1.7
Median				2.6
Interquartile range				2.2-2.8

Source: Municipal Yearbook, 1970.

EXHIBIT III-9

FIREMEN'S BENEFITS IN
SELECTED NEW JERSEY CITIES

CITY	BENEFITS			
	Average Annual Salary	Paid Vacation (Max. Days)	No. of Paid Holidays	Clothing Allowance
Atlantic City	$ 8,400	18	0	Yes
Orange	9,200	21	12	$100
Hackensack	9,825	16	6	$100
Plainfield	11,094	25	0	No
Irvington	10,000	-	8	$100
East Orange	9,200	28	-	$100
Bloomfield	9,600	20	6	$ 25
Union	10,000	24	4	$125
Rahway	10,000	25	12	$150

Source: Firemen's Benevolent Association, 1970.

alarms has increased 35 percent—from 1,035 in 1965 to 1,402 in 1969. This does not mean that there has been a large increase in fires; rather false alarms and school and civil disturbances (column 3) have added greatly to the work load.

Exhibit III-11 shows the increased personnel requirements and expenditures for 1966 to 1970 that have resulted from this increased demand for fire services.

As is the case with other city services, wages and salaries have increased more than the other items. The increase is due, in part, to the addition of nine men to the division, but the greater part of this increased expenditure is the result of higher wage demands prompted by

EXHIBIT III-10

ANALYSIS OF FIRE ALARMS

YEAR	(1) Total Alarms	(2) Actual Fires	(3) Alarms (Other Reasons)*
1965	1,035	702	333
1966	1,002	677	325
1967	1,123	745	378
1968	1,173	780	393
1969	1,402	862	540

Source: Annual Reports, Plainfield Fire Department.
*Other reasons include false alarms, smoke scares and accidental alarms.

EXHIBIT III-11

FIRE DEPARTMENT EXPENDITURES
1966-1970

YEAR	Number of Personnel Uniformed	Civilian	Wages & Salaries	Other Expenses*	Hydrant Rental	Total Expenditures
1966	115	1	$ 847,660	$53,185	$ 92,500	$ 993,345
1967	112	2	929,959	75,680	92,400	1,098,039
1968	114	2	1,029,173	59,612	97,193	1,185,978
1969	122	2	1,149,913	50,733	113,310	1,313,956
1970	122	3	1,333,696	59,272	117,630	1,510,598

Source: Annual Report, Plainfield Fire Department.

*Other expenses include communications, training and supplies for the division.

EXHIBIT III-12

COST PER ALARM ANSWERED

YEAR	COST PER ALARM
1966	$ 991
1967	978
1968	1,011
1969	937

Source: Plainfield Study, 1970.

the general inflation of the economy. When expenditures are viewed in terms of cost for each alarm answered, the result as Exhibit III-12 shows, is a slight decrease.

FUTURE NEEDS

Discussion within the department suggests a future growth in the number of personnel to 130 uniformed men, thereby adding eight new firemen to the budget at an approximate beginning salary of $8,500 (Exhibit III-13); in turn this would increase total wage and salary expenditures by $68,000. The reason for this increase in personnel is primarily the need for men to cover those on vacation; this added vacation coverage is due to the recent union contract which granted vacation benefits to firemen.

EXHIBIT III-13

FIRE DEPARTMENT PERSONNEL
AND THEIR SALARIES

POSITION	Salary Range	Number of Employees
Uniformed Staff		
Chief	$12,233-17,205	1
Deputy chief	12,003-15,603	4
Captain	10,887-14,151	9
Lieutenant	9,875-12,839	18
Fireman	8,530 11,094	88
Civilian Staff		
Administrative secretary	8,599	1
Senior typist	5,237	1
Clerk typist	4,524	0

Source: Plainfield Fire Department Records.

If funds are available, the recently organized fire patrol may be expanded. Since this program is new and experimental, no estimates of its future costs can be made.

The expense of training new men is likely to be small. The present turnover rate is 5 percent, with most retirements by firemen at higher salary levels. The approximately $2,500 training cost is, therefore, offset by the replacement of retired men with men at lower wage rates.

Changes outside of the department other than unpredictable civil crises will probably not significantly change the expenditure pattern in the five-year span of this report. In the longer run, however, new construction of high-rise apartments and conversions of older houses to multiple-family dwellings may increase the costs of coping with fire. If the new apartments are equipped with sprinkler systems, this will not be a problem, but unless conversions are tightly controlled by proposed zoning ordinances, more fires will occur.

PROJECTION OF FUTURE EXPENDITURES

The expenditures of the fire division will be generalized and divided into three categories: wages and salaries; other expenses; and hydrant rentals.

The first item, wages and salaries, grew both in dollar value and in the number of men staffing the force. In deriving its projected-rate-of-change value it is necessary to estimate the increases due to staff enlargement. Exhibit III-14 illustrates the average salary and its rate of growth. The probable addition of eight new firemen in 1971 can now be incorporated into the analysis, adding approximately $68,000 to the budget projection. Thereafter, the inflationary factor of 11.5 percent

EXHIBIT III-14

AVERAGE SALARY OF
FIRE DEPARTMENT PERSONNEL
(1966 TO 1970)

YEAR	AVERAGE SALARY
1966	$ 7,307
1967	8,157
1968	8,872
1969	9,273
1970	10,669

Source: Annual Report, Plainfield Fire Department.
Note: The average annual growth rate was 11.5 percent.

will increase the base figure to a new expenditure level in 1975. The result of these calculations is shown in Exhibit III-15.

The remaining two items (other expenditures and hydrant costs) will be treated in a simpler manner. Since there has been no abrupt change in the amounts supplied for either, the average rate of change over the past five years will be used as the projection rate. Exhibit III-15 displays the year-by-year projection based upon the above procedure.

* * *

The projection shows that total fire division expenditures will increase from the present appropriation of $1,511,000 to $2,635,000 assuming that inflationary trends continue through 1975.

DIVISION OF HEALTH

The changing character of Plainfield's residents has broadened the demands on the public health department. There has been a gradual shift, as the middle class is replaced by the poor, from health services secured through private physicians to the public hospitals. As the following material indicates, Plainfield shares this symptom with many older core cities.

The major functions of Plainfield's Division of Health are: environmental sanitation, which consists of inspecting all food-handling facilities (mainly restaurants); and the provision of maternal and child care to those who need it. The Visiting Nurse Association (VNA) has contracted to provide this care. The division of health is also responsible for issuing and registering vital statistics such as birth and marriage certificates, as well as responding to citizens' complaints concerning health.

Clinics of various types (the major one being dental) are operated in conjunction with school authorities. State funds are used to operate these clinics.

EXPENDITURE ANALYSIS

Clinics

At present there is a full-time staff of one health officer, two sanitary inspectors and three office workers. In addition, there are part-time positions for additional inspectors (plumbing), lab technicians, office workers and those needed for clinic operations (measles, immunization and the like).

The number of personnel has stayed relatively constant over the last few years although some positions have remained vacant. The 1969 budget shows the first significant salary jump due to an increment in

EXHIBIT III-15

PROJECTED FIRE DEPARTMENT EXPENDITURES

	Actual Appropriation for 1970	Percent Change	1971	1972	1973	1974	1975
Wages/salaries	$1,334	11.5%	$1,555*	$1,734	$1,933	$2,155	$2,403
Other expenses	59	2.9	61	63	65	67	69
Hydrant rental	118	6.8	126	134	143	153	163
Modified yearly projection	1,511		1,742	1,931	2,141	2,375	2,635

Source: Plainfield Study, 1970.

Note: Expenditure amounts are expressed in thousands of dollars.

*This value includes the cost of eight new men and an inflationary increment (see p. 000 of text).

personnel (Exhibits III-16 and III-17). The addition of two new part-time positions—a public health inspector and a medical inspector—are the cause of this increase.

Grants to Other Organizations

The other major items in the health budget are grants to Muhlenberg Hospital and payments to the VNA. City aid to the hospital rose from

EXHIBIT III-16

PERCENTAGE DISTRIBUTION OF
EXPENDITURES OF THE
DIVISION OF HEALTH (1965 TO 1970)

EXPENDITURE	1965	1966	1967	1968	1969	1970
Salaries	33.8%	31.4%	26.6%	27.6%	29.3%	32.6%
Clinics	0.0	0.0	2.4	9.7	12.2	16.1
Visiting nurse	25.2	23.7	24.3	21.4	20.3	19.6
Aid to Muhlenberg Hospital	35.9	41.7	44.4	38.8	36.0	25.7
Other	5.1	3.2	2.3	2.5	2.2	6.0
Total	100.0%	100.0%	100.0%	100.0%	100.0%	100.0%

Source: Financial Statements, City of Plainfield.

EXHIBIT III-17

EXPENDITURES OF THE DIVISION OF HEALTH
(1965 TO 1970)

EXPENDITURE	1965	1966	1967	1968	1969	1970
Salaries	$ 47	$ 49	$ 45	$ 54	$ 65	$ 75
Clinics			4	19	27	37
Visiting nurse	35	37	41	42	45	45
Aid to Muhlenberg Hospital	50	65	75	76	80	59
Other	7	5	4	5	5	14
Total	$139	$156	$169	$196	$222	$230

Source: Financial Statements, City of Plainfield.
Note: Expenditure amounts are expressed in thousands of dollars.

$50,000 in 1965 to $80,000 in 1969, with 70 to 80 percent of each yearly payment being used to pay for care of the indigent; the remainder was a donation to the hospital's expansion fund. Hospital assistance, with 66 percent slated for indigent care, dropped to $59,000 for 1970.

The amount of the contractual agreement with the VNA has risen from $35,000 in 1965 to $45,000 in 1970. The prime purpose of this contract is to provide maternal and child care to the indigent. Since the Model Cities Agency hopes to establish a permanent child care and maternity clinic, this operation could be phased out, but it is not known if such long-term financing can be anticipated. In the event that model cities funding was discontinued, responsibility would revert to the city. This is just one example of the build-up of municipal expenditures under external financing—with potential impact on the city's resources.

FUTURE NEEDS

The division director feels that one or two more inspectors will be needed within the next two years, and anticipates that a staff of six inspectors will be required eventually. This would permit the division to have two full-time food-establishment inspectors, one full-time plumbing inspector, an air-pollution inspector and two men to handle additional complaints.

The number of complaints has increased by about 30 percent a year over the last three years, probably because of the public's increased awareness of health problems—brought to their attention by federal programs such as model cities and the media publicity that environmental quality is now receiving.

The insect and rodent control program now being administered by the division of health in cooperation with the Model Cities Agency is an example of how federal programs can increase demands upon city agencies. Although the federal government is funding its own expenses and personnel, the Plainfield health officer spends about 30 percent of his time on this program. In addition, the public relations campaign which advertises this program has made many people aware of the existence of the division and its other duties.

Garbage collection, as noted in Exhibit III-18, is the cause of the most persistent complaint received by the division. (Notice in Chapter I the low rating given this area by Plainfield citizens.) At present, garbage is collected by 55 privately operated and licensed vehicles. The operators solicit the business of each household and commercial establishment of the city. This has resulted in a gradual and informal development of overlapping pick-up regions within the city.

The New Jersey Cartmen's Association, which represents the indi-

EXHIBIT III-18

**COMPLAINTS RECEIVED BY THE
BOARD OF HEALTH**

COMPLAINT	Number of Complaints (Jan. - Mar. 1970)	Percentage of Total Complaints
Garbage	107	49%
Animal bites	40	18
Seasonal		
No heat in winter; weeds, insects in spring-summer)	26	11
Rodents, etc.	30	14
Other	17	8
Total	220	100.0%

Source: Records of the Plainfield Division of Health.

vidual operators, does not serve as a centralized billing location. Records of garbage routes, payments, service levels and discontinued services are not maintained. The absence of this type of information center hinders the prompt pick-up of garbage from citizens unable or unwilling to pay for collection services by making it difficult for the division of health to find out that garbage is piling up and that a health hazard exists.

These problems indicate that the city may have to shed its passive participation in the garbage collection function. Increased participation could take the form of franchising collection routes throughout the city to private companies. Services which in an upper-middle-class suburb can be delegated to the private market become less satisfactory as the requirements of the city's inhabitants change. The poor require a much more substantial public infrastructure than do the rich.

Financing Future Needs

The additional manpower mentioned earlier can be obtained in two ways: additional funds; or reorganization of intradepartmental and, possibly, interdepartmental responsibilities.

The leveling-off of expenditures is not likely to continue (Exhibit III-19). Reorganization of duties and departments will only extend the grace period before additional funds are needed. As these funds will be needed to support programs dealing with regional problems such as air and water pollution, the city cannot bear the burden alone.

EXHIBIT III-19

PROJECTED EXPENDITURES OF THE
DIVISION OF HEALTH

	1970	Percent Change	1971	1972	1973	1974	1975
Salaries	$ 75	4.1%	$ 78	$ 81	$ 84	$ 88	$ 91
Visiting nurse service	45	6.5	48	51	54	58	62
Muhlenberg Hospital	59	3.5	61	63	65	68	70
Clinics	39	8.0	42	45	49	53	57
Other	14	4.1	15	16	16	17	18
Total Projected Expenditures	$232		$244	$256	$268	$284	$298

Source: Plainfield Study, 1970.
Note: Expenditure amounts are expressed in thousands of dollars.

Inflation will cause salary demands to rise to at least $91,000 by 1975 if present personnel levels are maintained. Moreover, if four additional inspectors are added to the payroll, as desired by the health officer, salary requirements will be in the neighborhood of $130,000.

The cost of the contract with the VNA is unlikely to increase much in the next five years. Model cities programs will deal with health problems among the increasing number of low-income residents, who at present receive a major share of VNA services. However, as medical costs have been continuously rising throughout the country, an increase of about $15,000 over the next five years can be anticipated based on past records. It is possible that the existence of alternate programs (model cities, welfare assistance, Muhlenberg Hospital) will keep costs from reaching this level.

With the transfer in 1970 of some responsibilities from Muhlenberg Hospital to welfare assistance, grants to the hospital are unlikely to approach the 1969 figure of $80,000 in the near future. Additional funds needed for indigent care will be supplied through welfare assistance. Assuming that yearly costs increase at about the same rate as in 1967 to 1969, the hospital grant will be $70,000 in 1975. As the clinics are completely funded by state funds, increases in clinic costs will not require additional outlays by the city.

WELFARE DEPARTMENT

The Plainfield Welfare Department has as its main function the distribution of money or purchase orders to persons whom the welfare director judges in need. The initial source of the assistance payments is the public assistance trust fund, which is budgeted by the city.

ELIGIBILITY

Eligibility for assistance is based on categories established in federal, state and county laws and policy. In addition, the Plainfield Welfare Department conditionally accepts all individuals adjudged needy who are not covered by another welfare program. (For data on welfare categories see Appendix C.) These include childless couples and single persons, as well as those who are either being processed by other governmental agencies or are emergency cases in need of help.

SOURCES OF WELFARE MONEY

Only those welfare programs not funded by state or county sources are left to be funded by the local tax base. Seventy-five percent of the verified hospital expenses paid out by the department for Medicaid patients are returned to the city's public assistance fund by the state department of welfare. The county welfare department at Elizabeth now administers several large welfare programs, among them the old age assistance program, the aid to dependent children (ADC) program and the disability assistance program. These programs are funded, in part, through a county tax levy added to the property tax base of each municipality.

COST ANALYSES

In analyzing the cost and performance data (Exhibits III-20 and III-21) one must first recognize the noncomparability of the data preceding January 1, 1969, with that following it, because on that date the ADC program was turned over to the county.

Keeping this data problem in mind, two findings emerge: 1) 1966 marked a low point in total persons served; both before and after 1966 a larger number of people were served with correspondingly higher costs; 2) administrative costs have increased relative to the number of persons served (Exhibit III-20, column 4).

One plausible reason given to explain the general pattern of aid expenditures is the unemployment level of the region. The number of insured unemployed in the Newark area (Exhibit III-22) shows a bottoming-out in the winter of 1966 which corresponds to the low in aid expenditures. Further agreement is seen in the present elevated levels (summer 1970) with increased aid expenditures.

The increase in administrative costs is caused predominantly by the

EXHIBIT III-20

ADMINISTRATIVE COSTS AND GROSS AID
EXPENDED BY THE WELFARE DEPARTMENT

YEAR	(1) Salaries/Wages	(2) Other Expenses	(3) Gross Aid Expended	(4) Administration costs per person served by municipal welfare
1963	$46,608.47	$4,214.56	$204,470.00	$ 9.17
1964	51,458.20	5,525.80	164,658.22	11.68
1965	53,631.93	4,990.15	158,782.14	15.78
1966	54,343.98	4,535.71	120,290.29	14.45
1967	63,429.32	5,010.37	156,257.29	12.72
1968	47,472.86	3,267.58	188,783.54	51.25
1969	60,502.00	1,510.00	56,862.26*	
1970 (appropriated)			70,234.00	

Source: Financial Statements, City of Plainfield.

Note: The formula used to calculate column (4) was:

$$\text{Administration costs per person served} = \frac{\text{Salaries, wages and other expenses}}{\text{Number of people served}}$$

*Shift of ADC cases pending approval to the Union County Welfare Board for direct payment.

EXHIBIT III-21

WORK LOAD OF THE WELFARE DEPARTMENT
(1963 TO 1970)

YEAR	Total Persons Served	Number of Applications Received	Number of Applications Accepted	Number of Cases Closed	Nonresidents of Plainfield
1963	6,958	811	561	601	658
1964	5,541	681	450	471	553
1965	4,880	623	438	453	474
1966	3,714	604	422	438	453
1967	4,075	651	471	433	717
1968	5,380	741	619	660	793
1969	990	533	391	396	134
1970 (August)	665		313	298	84

Source: Annual Reports, Plainfield Welfare Department.

EXHIBIT III-22

UNEMPLOYMENT IN THE NEWARK
LABOR AREA
(1963 TO 1970)

YEAR	AVERAGE NUMBER OF UNEMPLOYED
1963	23,000
1964	21,000
1965	17,000
1966	15,000
1967	16,000
1968	16,000
1969	16,000
1970 (projected)	19,000

Source: New Jersey Area Trends in Employment, Newark Labor Area,
Department of Labor and Industry, December 1970.

increased salary schedule of municipal employees. Notice that the number of staff members was 12 from 1963 to 1968. With the shift of the
ADC program to Union County the staff was cut back to seven; a year
and a half later (June 1970) one professional worker was added. Rather
than an increase in the number of personnel, the retention of higher-
salaried, more-experienced staff members and increases in their pay
have been the principal cause of the growth in administrative costs.

In addition, the size of welfare grants is increasing, partly because
increased costs of living mean larger allowances for each welfare
recipient, partly because of increased housing costs. Newcomers searching for housing in a low-vacancy housing market and local residents
facing loss of housing because of increased mortgage payments need
more financial aid than in the past.

PRESENT AND FUTURE DEPARTMENT NEEDS

The present and future needs of this department are related to the
physical plant in city hall, the operating policies of the county board,
and the level of unemployment and attractiveness of the city to lower-
income groups.

For the physical plant the most pressing present need is space for
both files and the secretary. Microfilming documents is one possible
solution. The present professional staff is adequate; however, a communication problem with the Union County office has resulted in some
duplications of welfare payments. An additional clerk might facilitate
communication.

We feel that future needs hinge too closely on regional economic
indicators to be forecast meaningfully. However, two trends should be

investigated through demographic analysis in conjunction with housing and employment availability: the change in the number of low-skilled and Spanish speaking people; and the change in the number of older people of all ethnic groups.

PROJECTED EXPENDITURES TO THE WELFARE DEPARTMENT

The projections for this department will be based upon three different patterns. The first pattern will be used to project the administrative aspects of the welfare department, including salaries and other expenditures. The pattern will begin with the legal changes of January 1969, which influenced both the work load and the total assistance payments.

The pattern will be formed by calculating the average salary of the department, finding its rate of change since the departmental reorganization, making the assumption that the present staff number will be continued through 1975 (Exhibit III-23). Then the increases in salary will be added to the base salary (1970). This will result in the 1971 to 1975 projected salary expenditure which is summarized in Exhibit III-24.

Calculation of other expenses will employ the projected change in the cost of living as measured by the CPI, adding the projected change onto expenses during the base year 1970. This value, as calculated elsewhere in this report (Exhibit II-1), is equal to an increase of 4.8 percent a year.

Besides administrative costs, the disbursement of public assistance must also be projected. This aspect of the department is highly correlated with unemployment; therefore, projections will be based on the assumption that unemployment levels will be constant.

EXHIBIT III-23

AVERAGE ANNUAL SALARY INFLATION
OF WELFARE DEPARTMENT EMPLOYEES

YEAR	Total Salaries	Number of Employees	Average Salary
1968	$63,429	12	$5,250
1969	47,472	7	6,714
1970	60,502	8	7,625

Source: Plainfield Study, 1970.

Note: The salary change for an average employee was calculated at 20.8 percent a year. This level of increase is undoubtedly due to the lower seniority staff bearing the brunt of the employee reduction. To correct for this, the inflated salary rate increase of the health department (4.1 percent) was used for calculations.

EXHIBIT III-24

PROJECTED WELFARE DEPARTMENT EXPENDITURES

EXPENDITURES	1970	Percent Change	1971	1972	1973	1974	1975
Administration salaries/wages	$ 61	4.1%	$ 64	$ 67	$ 70	$ 73	$ 76
Other expenses	1.5	4.8	2	2	2	2	2
Gross aid expended	110		115	121	127	133	139
Total projected expenditures	$173		$181	$190	$199	$208	$217

Source: See Exhibit III-20, p. 90.
Note: Expenditure amounts are expressed in thousands of dollars.

This procedure will allow a partial correction of a falling unemployment rate combined with what appears to be a slight influx of individuals initially without jobs. The calculation mechanism will be the projected change in the CPI of 4.8 percent a year. Exhibit III-24 summarizes each of these projections. It shows a peak expenditure of $217,000 in 1975.

PUBLIC LIBRARY

Public libraries are a classic rung in the ladder toward higher status. Exposure to a wider universe and encouragement of a self-help approach can give a child the inestimable gift of envisioning the world and his potential in it.

But the library must promote its wares to make the newcomer aware that he is welcome and that the library's resources may be valuable to him. This calls for money and staff far beyond what one would expect of an essentially passive resource. Additionally, since new suburban communities may have small library collections, older cities may have to provide services for their own populations plus groups of suburbanites.

A public library usually allocates its resources to three major areas: distributing library materials (books, records, films and so forth); assisting community groups; and serving as a reference source.

DISTRIBUTION OF MATERIALS

In the last five years the Plainfield Public Library has had to meet an increasing demand for nonfiction books from a collection that was formerly fiction oriented.

The designation of the Plainfield Public Library, in February 1969, as an area library in the state library system has reinforced this trend towards nonfiction. The library must now serve 20 surrounding library districts. Many of the industrial firms in the area request books from the Plainfield library, which can forward these requests to the Rutgers library if the book is not available in Plainfield. The interlibrary loan system and reader advisory and reference services have been the most rapidly growing services provided by the library, according to its director. The recent location of a branch of Union College in Plainfield will further increase the demand for reference services as well as interlibrary loan services.

The library's growth has been in services more related to its area role than its city role. The library cannot meet its increasing area demands as well as its community functions without more personnel and materials.

The library provided technical assistance to the school system when libraries were established in all the schools. At present, it aids the schools by sending personnel who provide library orientation and by encouraging class visits to the library.

The staff also prepares bibliographies on various topics. Among them are bibliographies of immediate value to the community, such as *How to Beat the High Cost of Living* and a recent list of election-oriented material.

In 1969, the library's collection of about 140,000 volumes had a circulation of 230,000, 70 percent of which was adult and young adult books. In addition, demands from school districts within the Plainfield area must be met from the Plainfield collection although assistance can be obtained from other libraries throughout the state. Most books circulate among the 23,000 registered borrowers (1,000 out-of-town families hold cards, with three members per family assumed) and are distributed as shown in Exhibit III-25.

Circulation Pattern

Over the last six years a considerable decline in the circulation pattern has been in progress, as shown in Exhibit III-26. (The completion of the new library building in 1968 and the six-week moving period required make the data for that year incompatible with that of the other years; thus, it has been excluded.) In 1970 there was a slight reversal in this trend, as a small increase in juvenile circulation produced about a 1 percent increase over the previous year in total circulation.

EXHIBIT III-25

DISTRIBUTION OF PUBLIC LIBRARY PATRONS

BORROWER GROUP	Number of Users (1969) (Approximate)	Percent
Adults and young adults	13,800	60%
Children	6,440	28
Out of town	2,760	12
Total	23,000	100.0%

Source: Annual Report, Plainfield Public Library.

EXHIBIT III-26

CIRCULATION OF PUBLIC LIBRARY MATERIALS

YEAR		MATERIALS	
	Total	Adult	Juvenile
1965	272,000	170,000	102,000
1966	260,000	168,000	92,000
1967	242,000	160,000	82,000
1968*	----	----	----
1969	230,000	166,000	64,000
1970	233,000	166,000	67,000

Source: Annual Reports, Plainfield Public Library.
*See p. 95 of text.

COMMUNITY ACTIVITIES

Community activity programs operated by the library make more use of library personnel than materials. Because of this, we have not made a breakdown of program costs. Activities of this type include summer clubs, adult and children's film and record programs, preschool and mothers' mind-stretching groups, and art and music exhibits arranged in conjunction with citizen groups. All of these are operated on an area-wide basis.

Although these activities encompass diverse areas, it is likely that most of the people who make use of them are already familiar with the library. At the present time, there are no active programs to attract those segments of the community that are underrepresented among library users. It is possible that few of the existing programs hold any interest for the city's minority groups. Perhaps programs on black history or English for the Spanish-speaking, carried on in cooperation with community groups and drawing on federal funds, should be considered for future expansion of library services to all segments of the community.

The library is responding to demographic change, albeit slowly because of the long-term nature of the changes needed. The library is aware of the increasing number of Spanish-speaking citizens in Plainfield. Spanish-language books (adult and juvenile) are now being included in library purchases. As a temporary measure, a number of Spanish-language books have been borrowed from the Newark library system. The library staff hopes that some future personnel will be fluent in Spanish, although the shortage of experienced library professionals relegates language proficiency to a secondary bargaining position.

REFERENCE

Use of the library premises by all segments of the Plainfield community has increased over the past few years even though total circulation has gone down. The pleasant atmosphere in the library, coupled with a reference section encompassing about 10 percent of the library's 140,000 volumes, has played a large role in this development. Exhibit III-27 illustrates how demand for reference services (especially telephone) has increased since the new library facilities became fully operational in 1969.

The population of Plainfield is relatively stable, while the population of surrounding communities is growing rapidly. Increasingly, therefore,

EXHIBIT III-27

DEMAND FOR REFERENCE SERVICE FROM THE LIBRARY

TIME PERIOD	Number of Reference Questions Asked in Library		Number of Telephoned Reference Questions	
	Total No.	Daily Average	Total No.	Daily Average
Oct. 1966 to June 1967 (old library)	1,704	48	381	12
Dec. 1968 to June 1969	1,639	48	973	29
Oct. 1969 to June 1970	3,154	60	2,143	41

Source: Annual Reports, Plainfield Public Library.

EXHIBIT III-28

PUBLIC LIBRARY APPROPRIATIONS
(1965 TO 1970)

EXPENDITURE	1965	1966	1967	1968	1969	1970
			YEAR			
Total	$175,637.24	$177,920.11	$203,597.76	$301,044.25	$299,572.02	$381,979.00
Materials	38,842.69	32,979.04	48,964.65	53,950.00	46,236.31	56,525.00
Utilities	4,173.75	4,348.92	4,056.08	21,150.00	18,798.20	19,700.00
Insurance/auditing	2,059.09	2,351.24	1,777.69	3,581.00	3,075.98	3,250.00
Heating	1,346.00	1,755.79	2,086.13	2,700.00	1,354.95	1,600.00
Bldg. maintenance	2,058.06	857.80	1,047.26	11,355.50	14,006.30	19,950.00
Library supplies	3,700.01	3,246.33	4,158.89	6,868.75	4,497.46	5,997.00
Office supplies	1,028.42	1,182.54	917.70	1,713.50	1,885.68	2,334.50
Bldg. supplies	574.26	581.42	382.17	1,219.50	1,453.62	2,203.00
Furniture & equip.	669.78	4,682.61	1,180.59	1,763.00	5,044.09	5,330.50
Miscellaneous	4,051.66	4,182.83	4,265.46	4,654.00	4,222.77	5,110.00
Subtotal	58,503.72	56,168.52	68,836.62	108,955.25	100,575.36	122,000.00
Salaries	117,133.52	121,751.59	134,761.14	192,089.00	191,896.66	259,979.00
State Aid — Area Union Serial Project	—	—	—	—	7,100.00	—

Source: Annual Reports, Plainfield Public Library.

the reference services are being used by non-Plainfieldites. The five additional reference librarians (there are now 11) needed by 1975, according to the library director, will be serving the library's entire service area rather than Plainfield alone. Requests for additional state funds are therefore justified by the increasing amount of time that will be devoted to non-Plainfield residents by the library staff.

FINANCIAL PICTURE

The major appropriations have been salaries, as shown in Exhibit III-28. To meet these higher levels, appropriation requests over the past five years have had to be increased by 50.1 percent. As Exhibit III-29 shows, much of this increase has been met by funds other than the city's.

Conversion of the Plainfield Public Library into an area library has caused a drop in out-of-town registration. Three years ago there were approximately 3,000 registered out-of-town users ($10 per family a year or $3 per family for 3 months), most of them holders of yearly cards. There are now only 1,000 registered out-of-town users. It is unlikely that many of the new residents settling in the towns around Plainfield will register, since they need not do so to use the library. This means a potentially large source of revenue will be denied. The argument broached earlier, that additional state funds are required if the Plainfield Public Library is to operate as an area library without impairing its local role, is strengthened by the loss of revenue mentioned above.

Federal funds have been tapped whenever possible. The Federal Public Library Service and Construction Act (P.L. 88-269) has been the source of these funds. Title I funds from this act were utilized by the library in providing assistance to the Neighborhood House in building up a library collection. Title II funds were used in the construction of the present library facilities which opened in 1968.

The expected amount of federal funds did not materialize in 1969, which led to a cut in expenditures for library material. This probably added a year to the library's period of maturation, as purchases that were needed in order to provide full service had to be delayed. Small as the federal contribution was, its temporary termination had a noticeable effect upon library service. The fragility of the library's financial structure and its need for assured funds is amply demonstrated by this incident.

FUTURE NEEDS OF THE PUBLIC

Federal funds, which are to be used in providing or improving public library services, might provide the means to study how service to the community could be improved. The significance of this study would lie

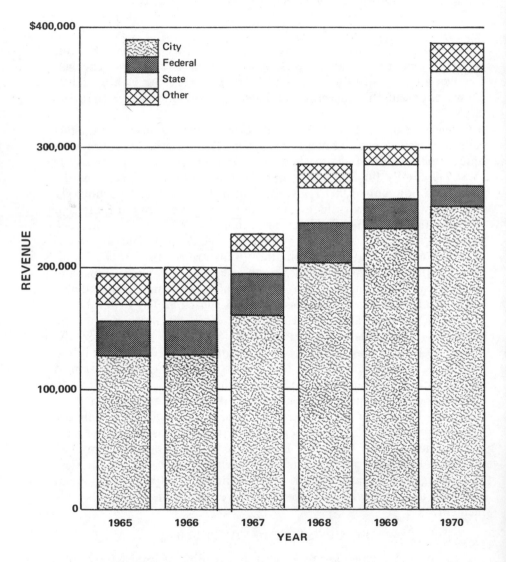

EXHIBIT III-29
PUBLIC LIBRARY APPROPRIATIONS, 1965-1970

Source: Financial Statement, City of Plainfield

in its recommendations concerning future capital costs. The location of the library, although convenient to motorists, is a great handicap to public transit users. When bus service is available (the last return bus passes the library at about 6:30 PM), those travelling to the East End or West End must transfer. The trip is costly (50 cents one way) as well as inconvenient.

A branch library in the East End was closed upon completion of the present building. This was done in order to save money, and because the opening of school libraries lessened the demands made upon the branch, which had primarily served children. The volumes in the school libraries, however, are not available to the public. Furthermore, it is unlikely that they are as extensive in scope as those in the local library were.

A library has been set up in the Neighborhood House but it can only be considered a temporary solution to service in the West End. However, the MCA is contemplating the establishment of a minibus operation to provide service to Muhlenberg Hospital. Since its route would pass the library, it might be used to serve library as well as hospital users. The MCA might also provide a means for expansion of library services, for instance, through the construction of a library in the proposed Manpower Training Center.

At the present time, the library shows large deficiencies in only two of the 66 guidelines established by the American Library Association's *Minimum Standards for Public Library Systems*. These are easy accessibility and service to all the city's groups.

FUTURE NEEDS OF THE LIBRARY

If the library staff is to be maintained at present levels for the next five years, salary expenditures will increase to approximately $370,000 based on the rate of increase prior to staffing of the new building (Exhibit III-30). Moreover, if the staff is increased to the size deemed necessary by the library director, salary costs will be in the neighborhood of $500,000 by 1975, due to a 50 percent increase in professional personnel.

Material expenditures, which now amount to $56,525, could be predicted to drop to lower levels as soon as the library is through with its expansion program. The additional duties that the library has assumed as an area library, however, make it reasonable to predict that material expenditures cannot drop below the $50,000 level without impairing services. The greater use of library materials will increase costs such as binding and rebinding. A figure of $55,000 has therefore been used as representative of material costs in the next five years.

EXHIBIT III-30

EXPENDITURE PROJECTIONS FOR THE PUBLIC LIBRARY (1971 TO 1975)

EXPENDITURE	Increment Factor	Base Sum	1971	1972	1973	1974	1975
Salaries*	7.3%	$259,929	$278,904	$299,264	$321,110	$344,551	$369,703
Materials	0.0	56,525	55,000	55,000	55,000	55,000	55,000
Other	8.9	65,475	71,302	77,648	84,559	92,085	100,280
Total		$381,929	$405,206	$431,912	$460,669	$491,636	$524,983

Source: Plainfield Study, 1970.
*Present staff number plus five additional members (see p. 101 of text).

EXHIBIT III-31

DIVISION OF RECREATION EXPENDITURES (1965 TO 1970)

EXPENDITURE	YEAR					
	1965	1966	1967	1968	1969	1970
Salaries	$105,000	$110,000	$123,000	$147,000	$153,000	$190,000
Other expenses	18,000	16,000	19,000	33,000	24,000	29,000
Total	$123,000	$126,000	$142,000	$180,000	$177,000	$219,000

Source: Financial Statements, City of Plainfield.

The "other" category, which includes items such as heating insurance and building maintenance, is relatively stable. Insurance, utility and heating costs, however, are subject to unpredictable variations; an increment factor of 5 percent has been used in projecting these costs to 1975.

Until the state decides on the future role of the area library, the above estimates must be considered extremely flexible.

DIVISION OF RECREATION

The Plainfield Division of Recreation is responsible for providing and maintaining facilities required for recreational and leisure-time use by all age groups. Supervisory personnel are provided for many of these activities, such as swimming, adult tennis, golf leagues and so forth. Some of the activities are supported cooperatively with the board of education.

PRESENT FACILITIES AND PERSONNEL

The major public facilities provided by the division of recreation are four playgrounds and three swimming pools. The Plainfield Avenue Playground is also the site of a year-round indoor center. In addition, there is an agreement with the board of education to allow use of its facilities during the summer months.

In cooperation with the board of education, an adult education evening school is sponsored for residents and nonresidents of Plainfield. This is a nonprofit community enterprise carried out with the assistance of the Plainfield Adult Education Advisory Council.

EXPENDITURES

Divisional expenditures jumped in 1968, and have remained at rather high levels since then (Exhibit III-31). The increase in expenditures between 1967 and 1968 resulted from responses to the racial disturbances of 1967 in Plainfield. A permanent pool was built in 1967-1968 in the West End and greatly inflated the "other expenses" category for 1968. In addition, two portable pools have been obtained over the past two years.

For the most part, however, salaries have been the most significant factor in costs. There are two major categories of personnel: full-time, who received about two-thirds of total salaries for 1970; and irregular or seasonal personnel. Salaries of additional personnel working in summer programs caused much of the increased salary expenditure for 1968 and 1969.

Because federal monies helped finance the swimming pools, pool usage cannot be limited to Plainfield residents. Furthermore, some of the activities supervised by the division of recreation are open to non-Plainfield residents.

The Plainfield Division of Recreation, like the Plainfield Public Library, is supplying services to surrounding communities without adequate compensation for operational expenses.

FUTURE NEEDS AND EXPENDITURES

The department anticipates increased pressure on existing facilities, but it does not include construction of any facilities other than swimming pools and vest-pocket parks among realizable goals within the next five years. The major expense factor over the next five years will thus continue to be salaries (Exhibit III-32). Inflationary pressures will push them to about $231,000.

EXHIBIT III-32

**PROJECTED EXPENDITURES FOR THE
DEPARTMENT OF RECREATION**

EXPENDITURE	1970	Percent Change	1971	1972	1973	1974	1975
Salaries	$190	4%	$198	$206	$214	$222	$231
Other	29	-20	35	42	50	60	72
Total projected expenditures	$219		$233	$248	$264	$282	$303

Source: Plainfield Study, 1970.
Note: Expenditure amounts are expressed in thousands of dollars.

The increment factor used in salary projections was based upon the two years in which division responsibilities had stabilized. A large increment factor was used in projecting "other expenses" in the event that new facilities would have to be built with a large share of city funds. In addition, we felt that costs for additional personnel needed to staff new facilities should be included in this large increment.

An entirely new expense may be incurred if the board of education follows through on its threat to impose rental fees for use of its facilities. This action, however, would have no effect upon the overall city budget, as these fees could be deducted from board of education appropriations and alloted to the division of recreation.

The construction of a new swimming pool and vest-pocket parks are the only major capital expenses likely to occur within the next five years. The cost for a large community pool would be at least $200,000, meaning that construction cannot even be considered without a firm guarantee of outside assistance. Costs for vest-pocket parks are difficult to determine as the property is obtained when it becomes available.

Thus, an emergency appropriation of about $30,000 was made in 1970 in order to purchase some property near the Mathewson Playground for a vest-pocket park. Four additional vest-pocket parks are now under consideration. It is hoped that Federal Urban Beautification funds will be available to help defray some of the required costs.

* * *

For the most part, increases in expenditures will result from increasing salary demands. However, even if outside funds are made available to the city, additional local funds would still be needed to finance any swimming pool or park projects undertaken.

AGGREGATED EXPENDITURES

The preceding six fiscal studies concerned departments whose size and clear-cut functions allowed their individual treatment. The remaining budgeting departments have been grouped within their major divisional headings.

These expenditure items have been grouped into four budget categoies: general government; administration and finance; public works and urban development; and public affairs and safety and miscellaneous accounts.

In each case, the level of expenditures taken from the official financial statement is traced through the years 1965 to 1970; following this, projected expenditure levels are generated based upon the preceding rate of change in expenditures.

GENERAL GOVERNMENT

The various items included under this budget subheading have been grouped into two categories. The first is city operations. This category contains the group of expenditure items that support the overall legislative and administrative function. Specifically, these items are the city council, the city administrator, the mayor, the corporation council and municipal insurance. The second category subsumed under the general government budget subheading is public operations. This category contains two functions funded by the federal government. The items are the community action program and the human relations division.

City operations expenditures will continue to climb over the next five years, since insurance premiums (the major item in this category) show no sign of a slowdown. The city administrator item introduced in 1970 is the only new budget item in this group. The council and mayor items

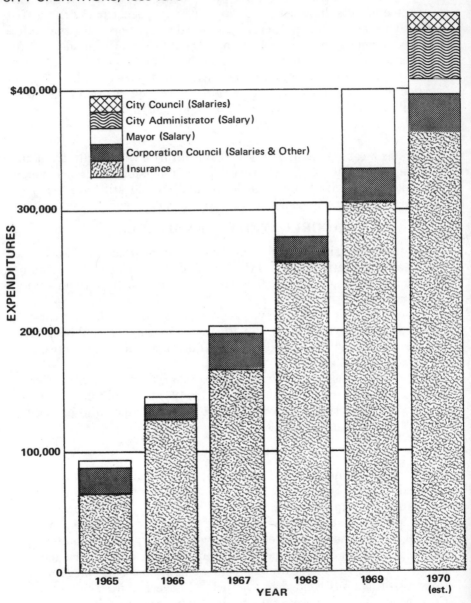

EXHIBIT III-33
GENERAL GOVERNMENTAL EXPENDITURES:
CITY OPERATIONS, 1965-1970

EXPENDITURES

$400,000

300,000

200,000

100,000

0

City Council (Salaries)
City Administrator (Salary)
Mayor (Salary)
Corporation Council (Salaries & Other)
Insurance

1965 1966 1967 1968 1969 1970
(est.)

YEAR

III — 33
Source: Financial Statements, City of Plainfield.

are shown in Exhibit III-33 combined in the item entitled "Administration and Executive Office of the Mayor and Governing Body through 1969." Increases in items other than insurance will probably be due to salary increases based on longevity.

Projection of General Governmental Expenditures

For purposes of projection this expenditure item must be broken down into three subdivisions: insurance, salaries for city operations and expenditures for public operation.

Exhibit III-33 shows a dramatic increase in these items, largely as a result of insurance premiums and rate changes. The last major rise in these costs occurred following the civil unrest of 1967; since then, the indication is that the premium payments are slowly beginning to stabilize. Further increases will be due to inflationary rate increases allowed by the state and the assumption under state law of all medical insurance payments for municipal employees by the city. Therefore, in estimating the rate of increase, the inflationary change from 1969 to 1970 will be projected for the next five years; this value is a 16 percent increase per year.

The second subdivision involves the governmental reorganization of 1969. The rate of change under the new organizational structure has been used rather than the relative increase over the last five years. Annual increases in this area are at the 5 percent level.

Last, the public operations subdivision which administers to federal projects will probably continue to grow. The inflation value reflecting the growth over the last three years is 10.8 percent per year (Exhibit III-34).

Exhibit III-35 displays the results of these calculated projections. It shows that the present level of expenditures of $530,000 will increase by 90 percent over the projection period to a new value of $994,000.

DEPARTMENT OF ADMINISTRATION AND FINANCE

The department of administration and finance contains those budget items which maintain the finance and tax collection functions. The budget items included in this category are the director of administration and finance, the division of administration, the department of public buildings and grounds, the city clerk, the treasury, the assessor and the department of audit and control.

The costs of maintaining these programs are shown on Exhibit III-36.

Expenditure Projections

For purposes of projecting expenditures the various items included in the budget statement for this department[1] have been classified under

EXHIBIT III-34

**GENERAL GOVERNMENTAL EXPENDITURES:
PUBLIC OPERATIONS, 1965-1970**

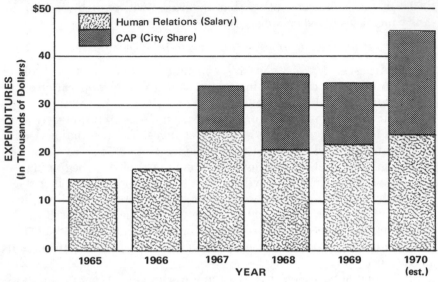

Source: Financial Statement, City of Plainfield

EXHIBIT III-35

**PROJECTED EXPENDITURES FOR
GENERAL GOVERNMENT [a]**

CITY OPERATION	1970	Percent Change	1971	1972	1973	1974	1975
Insurance[b]	$360	16.0%	$418	$485	$563	$653	$757
Salaries/other [c]	125	5.0	131	138	145	152	160
Public operation [d]	45	10.8	50	56	62	69	77
Total projected expenditures	$530		$599	$679	$770	$874	$994

Source: See Exhibit III-33, p. 106.

Note: Expenditure amounts are expressed in thousands of dollars.

[a] Items included in the following categories were derived from the Corporation Notice, City of Plainfield, 1970 Local Municipal Budget.

[b] Insurance includes group insurance for employees, surety, bond premiums and other insurance premiums. For comparable cost increments see Sternlieb, The Urban Housing Dilemma, New York, 1970.

[c] Salaries and other expenses include mayor, city council, city administration operation council and leased land payments.

[d] Public Operations include the human relations commission and Aid to Community Action, Plainfield, Inc.

EXHIBIT III-36

GENERAL GOVERNMENTAL EXPENDITURES
FOR THE DEPARTMENT OF ADMINISTRATION
AND FINANCE

YEAR	EXPENDITURES
1965	$157,000
1966	166,000
1967	174,000
1968	189,000
1969	214,000
1970	257,000

Source: Financial Statements, City of Plainfield.

two categories: salaries and other (Exhibit III-37). These are assumed to increase with the same inflationary pressure as the general governmental group. This value will be assumed to be a 5 percent a year increase for both salaries and other expenses.

Thus, a 28 percent increase in expenditures is projected over the next five years.

DEPARTMENT OF PUBLIC WORKS AND URBAN DEVELOPMENT

The department of public works and urban development, reorganized within the past two years, includes a variety of functions relating to the planning, rebuilding and maintenance of the city's physical plant. The director's salary is divided among the budgets of his several divisions. He has delegated authority to several division heads (Exhibit III-38).

The divisions within this department are readily grouped into the four categories described below. 1) urban development—the administration of federal programs such as the model cities program and neighborhood development program, both of which are described elsewhere; 2) regulatory functions—the promulgation and enforcement of the legal constraints which affect the city's physical plant; 3) interdepartmental functions—the development and administration of the programs the public sees implemented via the divisions in the fourth category; 4) public functions—the provision of physical services to the city.

Urban Development

This division was staffed within the past six months under funds supplied to the Neighborhood Development Program (NDP), a federal

EXHIBIT III-37

EXPENDITURE PROJECTION: DEPARTMENT OF ADMINISTRATION AND FINANCE

	1970	Percent Change	1971	1972	1973	1974	1975
Salaries	$213,000	5%	$224,000	$235,000	$247,000	$259,000	$272,000
Other	91,000	5	96,000	101,000	106,000	111,000	116,000
Total projected expenditures	$304,000		$320,000	$336,000	$353,000	$370,000	$388,000

Source: Financial Statements, City of Plainfield.

program. The local share (25 percent) is currently paid with noncash credits. There are enough accrued credits from the locally financed library and high school projects to carry the local share of the NDP program to 1975.

The director foresees the city government continuing the renewal function after this time. Some cash outlay may be necessitated, but since no projects have yet been planned, the amount of the local share cannot be predicted now. Furthermore, the impossibility of determining the availability of future federal funds compounds the projection problem.

The salary payroll is currently running at $6,000 a month, according to the director, with total expenses approaching $100,000 for the 12-month period beginning August 1969.

The Aid to City Demonstration Agency is a new division with, as of June 1970, no expense entries. It is expected that requests from MCA for special city services will be honored and charged into this account.

Regulatory Functions

The code enforcement division administers the federal code enforcement program (essentially building inspection), and employs a relocation officer who helps to relocate families displaced by enforcement activities. Over the past five years this division has displayed a constant increase in both salaries and functions.

The past five-year increase of 141 percent in expenses will probably not be duplicated in the next five years, as many of the areas now inspected by this division will come within areas included in future phases of the NDP.

Board of Adjustment. This organization deals with granting variances to the zoning code. There has been essentially no change in expenses under this item over the past five years, and no major changes are contemplated over the next five years (Exhibit III-39).

Interdepartmental Functions

The director of public works has the responsibility for coordinating and supervising the activities of this department and advising the city administrator on administrative matters. It is unlikely that there will be any major monetary changes in this item.

The division of public works includes the various subdivisional maintenance crews. Costs assigned to this heading are essentially office and janitorial supplies, and utility expenses for all buildings housing maintenance equipment. These expenses have shown no extraordinary increases outside of inflation and normal utility rate hikes, and are unlikely to do so.

EXHIBIT III-38
DEPARTMENTAL DIVISIONS: DEPARTMENT OF PUBLIC WORKS & URBAN DEVELOPMENT

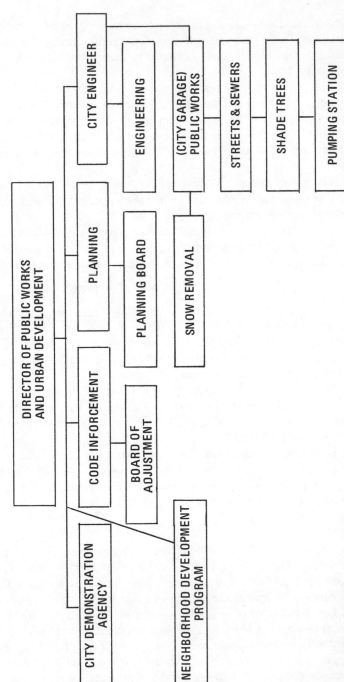

Source: Office of Director, Public Works,

The city garage has the responsibility for providing care, service, repair and maintenance of motor and nonmotor vehicles and equipment, and for maintaining and operating activities of the city facility. Prior to the recent reorganization, each department had to allocate funds for these items. It is hoped that maintenance expenses will be held down through the establishment of a common service area. Costs in this area are, however, likely to rise due to inflation.

The division of planning is responsible for: developing and preparing urban renewal programs for the city; maintaining a mechanism for continual review of the city's eligibility for federal and state aid programs; providing staff services, other than legal, to the planning board and board of adjustment; compiling and analyzing socioeconomic data and serving as a repository of information regarding land-use and population densities; and performing studies for use in formulating recommendations with respect to the physical development and needs of the city.

This division has been in existence for five years. Its staff has recently been expanded to include two full-time professionals and one secretary. Although a comprehensive development plan was recently completed, the consultant's fees were charged to the mayor's office prior to governmental reorganization. No staff additions are contemplated for the foreseeable future.

EXHIBIT III-39

DEPARTMENT OF PUBLIC WORKS EXPENDITURES,
REGULATORY FUNCTIONS, 1965-1970

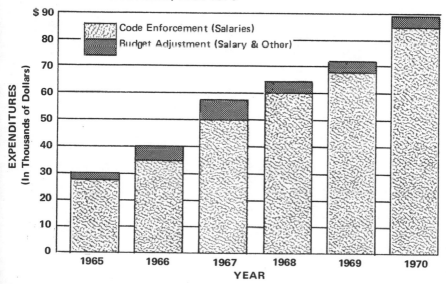

Source: Financial Statements, City of Plainfield.

The division of engineering has the responsibility for: providing professional engineering services as required by the department; maintaining maps, charts, plans, specifications, and records of public works facilities and utilities within the city; supervising the performance of public works contracts for the city and authorizing progress payments for such work.

The major cost item in this division (salaries to the professional staff) has remained fairly stable in the past five years. The staff has designed and managed some minor reconstruction projects recently, such as the City Hall parking lot. The city engineer does not anticipate any staff additions in the near future (Exhibit III-40).

Public Functions (Exhibit III-41)

Under the item labelled "Pumping Station" are allocations for maintaining and operating the pumping stations that keep city sewage flowing into the Middlesex Joint Sewage Disposal. A five-year history indicates that salary longevity and utility hikes were the major cost increase factors. Prior to 1970, these expenses were not budgeted separately.

The city engineer feels both plants are obsolete and will require replacement, at a total cost of $60,000, within the next five years. Except

EXHIBIT III-40

DEPARTMENT OF PUBLIC WORKS, INTERDEPARTMENTAL
FUNCTION EXPENDITURES, 1965-1970

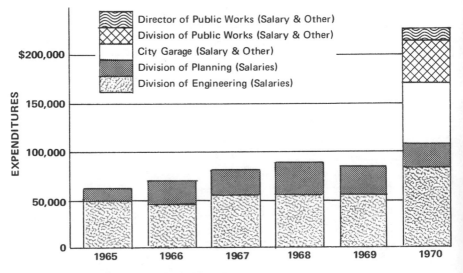

Source: Financial Statements, City of Plainfield

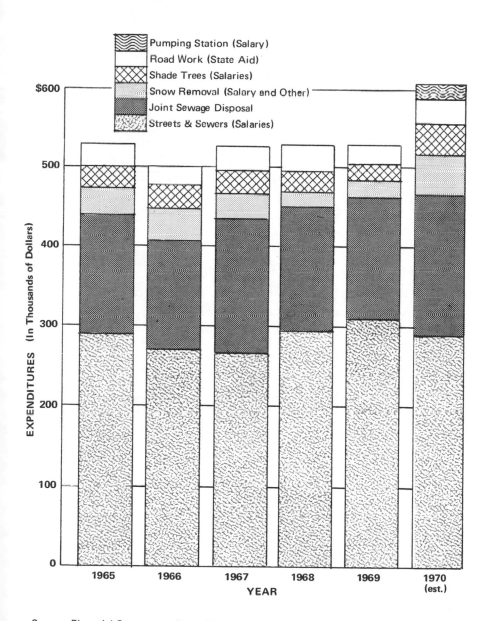

EXHIBIT III-41

DEPARTMENT OF PUBLIC WORKS EXPENDITURES,
PUBLIC FUNCTIONS, 1965-1970

Pumping Station (Salary)
Road Work (State Aid)
Shade Trees (Salaries)
Snow Removal (Salary and Other)
Joint Sewage Disposal
Streets & Sewers (Salaries)

EXPENDITURES (In Thousands of Dollars)

YEAR

Source: Financial Statements, City of Plainfield

EXHIBIT III-42

PROJECTED EXPENDITURES OF THE DEPARTMENT OF PUBLIC WORKS

	1970	Percent Change	1971	1972	1973	1974	1975
Total expenditures	$1,060,000	5%	$1,113,000	$1,169,000	$1,227,000	$1,288,000	$1,352,000

Source: Financial Statements, City of Plainfield.

EXHIBIT III-43

DEPARTMENT OF PUBLIC AFFAIRS & SAFETY, EXPENDITURES, POLICE & TRAFFIC FUNCTIONS, 1965-1970

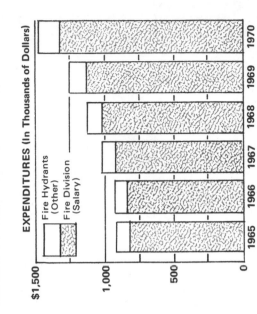

EXHIBIT III-44

DEPARTMENT OF PUBLIC AFFAIRS & SAFETY, EXPENDITURES, FIRE PROTECTION, 1965-1970

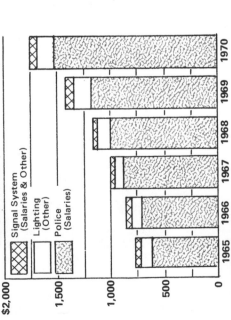

Source: Financial Statements, City of Plainfield

for these capital costs, this budget item is unlikely to increase significantly. It is hoped that the funds necessary for the new stations will be obtained from one of the new federal and state programs being developed to deal with environmental problems.

The road work budgetary item is concerned with the maintenance of state roads using state funds. No major changes can be anticipated until a new federal road policy is developed which would determine the amount of funds that states will have available for their minor road systems.

The shade tree bureau has the responsibility for maintaining and planting various flora on developed city property. The recent reorganization combined the beautification committee with the shade tree bureau. The purpose of this committee is to advise the mayor and city council, as well as Plainfield citizens, on how to maintain and improve the esthetic appeal of Plainfield.

Salary expenditures for shade tree personnel have decreased over the past five years in an effort to hold the overall budget line. However, beautification committee costs rose from zero to over $6,000 in 1970.

The city engineer indicated that an increase in work-load and expenses for this bureau would be desirable. Federal funds from the Urban Beautification Program may be used to defray some of these costs.

Over a five-year period (1965-1970) snow removal has cost the city amounts ranging from $42,000 in 1966 to a low of $18,967 in 1968. The cost of snow removal is primarily a function of snowfall and thus is prone to wide yearly fluctuations regardless of inflationary trends. In the long run, costs will tend to increase, but it is difficult to make any firm projection.

The joint sewage disposal account includes service charges for the connection to the Middlesex Joint Sewage Disposal. These charges will continue to increase gradually over the next five years, but will not be a major factor in increasing city expenditures.

The division of streets and sewers is responsible for maintaining and repairing all improved and accepted streets; maintaining, cleaning and repairing city storm and sanitary sewers; maintaining and cleaning all waterways and drainage ditches crossing land controlled by the city; maintaining and repairing street name signs. This division has had a relatively stable budget during the past five years. The city engineer has devised a street improvement program with total expenditures of a little over $2 million. He feels that improved streets will lower maintenance costs. The city engineer has indicated that rebuilding of major sewer mains may be necessary within a 10-year period due to their age (some date to the latter part of the nineteenth century).

At the present time, the NDP will be able to finance some of the required street and sewer improvements. There will probably be additional state and federal programs in the next few years to help defray costs. The city will be unable to undertake these improvements without aid of some sort.

Fiscal Overview

Of the four groups, the greatest impact upon expenditures will probably be in the public function category. The expenditures needed to up-

EXHIBIT III-45
DEPARTMENT OF PUBLIC AFFAIRS & SAFETY, EXPENDITURES HEALTH & WELFARE FUNCTIONS, 1965-1970

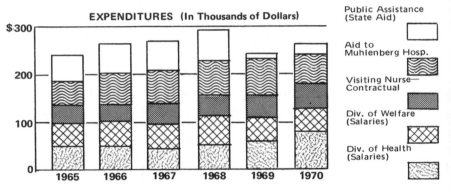

Source: Financial Statements, City of Plainfield

EXHIBIT III-46
DEPARTMENT OF PUBLIC AFFAIRS & SAFETY, EXPENDITURES, ADMINISTRATION & COURT, 1965-1970

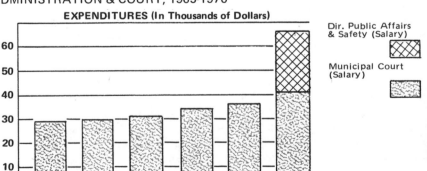

Source: Financial Statements, City of Plainfield

grade existing streets, sewers and pumping facilities will amount to $2 million for streets alone.

Urban development activities will require increasing amounts of money, but these costs will be insignificant relative to the costs of physical improvements for the city. The funds allocated to urban development activities will probably result in a saving of money for the city as these programs will cover some of the required expenditures as mentioned earlier.

As discussed above, the sharp rise in expenditures that paralleled the governmental reorganization and initiation of projects has largely subsided, allowing use of the 5 percent inflation figure used for the general governmental and administration and finance departments. Exhibit III-42 displays the projected expenditures for this department; they will increase about 28 percent during the time period analyzed.

PUBLIC AFFAIRS AND SAFETY

In an attempt to determine which functions draw most heavily upon city funds, activities of the department of public affairs and safety were divided into functional groups.

The police division and the bureau of signal system and street lighting are included in the police and traffic function. The division of fire and fire hydrants are included in the fire protection function. The function which encompasses administration and court expenditures includes funding for the director of public affairs and safety, and municipal court expenses.

Included in the health and welfare function are those items which directly affect the health and welfare of many Plainfield residents: public assistance aid to Muhlenberg Hospital; VNA contract; division of welfare; division of health.

Exhibits III-43 and III-44 demonstrate the increasing cost of supplying police and fire protection to Plainfield residents. The major items in both these areas are salaries.

Exhibit III-45 is surprising in that it shows no great upward trend in the area of health and welfare functions. Administrative and court expenditures (Exhibit III-46) are unlikely to change much in the next five years, although longevity increases will result in a gradual upward trend in this area.

Projected Expenditures

The preceding discussion regarding the department of public affairs and safety included within it several items that had previously been given more extensive treatment. These, therefore, will not be repeated

EXHIBIT III-47

PROJECTED EXPENDITURES FOR MISCELLANEOUS MUNICIPAL LINE ITEMS

EXPENDITURE	Appropriations 1970	Percentage Change	1971	1972	1973	1974	1975
Public affairs							
Salaries	$ 25	5%	$ 26	$ 27	$ 28	$ 29	$ 30
Other	4	5	4	4	4	4	4
Municipal court							
Salaries	42	20	50	60	72	84	101
Other	7	5	7	7	7	7	7
Street lighting	132	9	144	157	171	186	203
Signal system							
Salaries	42	20	50	60	72	84	101
Other	34	14	39	44	50	57	65
Civil defense	5	5	5	5	5	5	5
State law enforcement	9	5	9	9	9	9	9
Unclassified	263	9	287	313	341	372	405
Contingency	10	5	10	11	11	12	12
Capital improvements	13	0	13	13	13	13	13
Municipal debt service	299		293	289	282	276	276
Deferred charges and statutory payments	842	15	968	1,113	1,280	1,472	1,692
Interest on school debt	920	–2	902	884	866	849	832
Reserved for uncollected taxes	986	19	1,173	1,396	1,661	1,977	2,353
Total projected expenditures	$3,633		$3,980	$4,392	$4,872	$5,436	$6,108

Source: Plainfield Study, 1970.
Note: Amounts expressed are in thousands of dollars.

for the expenditure projection. There remain 14 items to be listed to complete the present appropriation list. This includes the remainder of the department of public affairs and safety and the very significant accounting categories which include statutory payments to employee retirement funds and the reserve for uncollected taxes. Exhibit III-47 lists these items and projects their dollar value through 1975.

There are three items unique in this study, in that expenditures are not expected to increase. These are the municipal and local school district debt services and capital improvements. It should be noted that while no new projects are anticipated through 1975, pressure for additions could mount.

The first nine items in Exhibit III-47 contain the remaining items for the department of public affairs and safety. The expenditure increases are based upon the previous five-year expenditure pattern and justified by either monetary inflation or, in the cases of the signal system and municipal court, the need for a professional level of service.

The two large categories that remain are increasing at a rapid rate but for different reasons. First, the deferred charges and statutory payments category is influenced most by the increased retirement benefits granted to municipal employees through state-required agreements; this has been increasing by about 15 percent a year.

The final category showing both rapid increases and large size is the reserve for uncollected taxes. The dollar value as estimated by the finance department is the amount required to cover tax payments defaulted by citizens. Two factors are influencing the size of this category: the increase in the percentage of citizens unable to pay their property tax; and the increasing size of the tax levy. We estimate the combined results to be a yearly increase of 19 percent in the reserve required to meet the following year's expenditures.

* * *

This concludes the analysis of the departments of municipal government in terms of their past expenditure patterns. In Chapter V each department's expenditure size and pattern will be considered, as modified by certain nonrecurring factors, and the expenditure required by each to maintain its present level of service will be projected.

FOOTNOTES

1. Corporation Notice, City of Plainfield, 1970 Local Municipal Budget.

Chapter IV

THE CHALLENGE OF EDUCATION

Education is the great common denominator of our society, the essential guarantee of social and economic mobility. One of the principal appeals of the zone of emergence to the upwardly mobile central-city émigré is the improved quality of the school system which he expects to find there. In turn, one of the principal challenges to the older suburb is the maintenance and improvement of standards so that it can meet these expectations.

The educational system of the older suburb is particularly subject to the strains of our time: the increasing breadth of educational requirements, the broadening of the pupil base particularly at the lower grade levels, the sudden questioning of hitherto positive attitudes and judgments of the efficacy of schools and the adequacy of their staffs.

Moreover, the Plainfields of the United States must cope with new students who often come ill prepared from the educational establishments of the central cities. The tests of reading readiness and the like given to new students underline their remedial needs. What is required, therefore, is an ever-increasing degree of effort. It is essential that the challenges of today and tomorrow be met, and that the sins of the past be countered. In this chapter some of the details of Plainfield's educational needs and expenditures are explored from a fiscal point of view.

The city of Plainfield operates a 15-plant school system. Fourteen of the schools house kindergarten through ninth grade, while one houses all high school students. The high school, opened in 1970, was designed to include all high school students—those enrolled both in academic as well as vocationally oriented programs.

At the present time eight schools serve kindergarten through fourth grade and two schools serve fifth and sixth grade. Two schools are for special education. There are two junior high schools and a new high school in addition to the old building.

As with all public schools the taxpayers of the city constitute the major support of the economic structure of the school system. During the 1969-1970 year, approximately 56 percent of the municipal tax dollar went to education. The system is also subsidized by state and federal aid. Several of the schools' major programs are funded either in part or totally through assistance programs. For example, through the Beadleston Act, the state reimburses the school system for 50 percent of the expenditures for the 251 students presently enrolled in the special education program. But before looking at the fiscal impacts of the system the focus must be on the students—their number and its implications.

THE STUDENTS

NUMBER

The cost of maintaining a school system depends mainly on the number of students and types of enrollment. In this section the emphasis will be upon numbers and the potential for expanded enrollment.

The total public school enrollment, as shown in Exhibit IV-1, has hovered around 9,200 pupils over the last seven years. The problem is to determine whether there are any constant trends within this slightly erratic total change pattern.

Exhibit IV-2 shows the absolute enrollment figures by grade for the

EXHIBIT IV-1

PLAINFIELD PUBLIC SCHOOL ENROLLMENT

YEAR	Total Enrollment	Percentage Change
1964 to 1965	9,270	
1965 to 1966	9,140	−1.4%
1966 to 1967	8,998	−1.6
1967 to 1968	9,108	1.2
1968 to 1969	9,171	0.7
1969 to 1970	9,083	−1.0
1970 to 1971	9,338	2.8

Source: Records, Office of the Assistant to the Superintendent, Plainfield School District.

EXHIBIT IV-2

PLAINFIELD PUBLIC SCHOOL ENROLLMENT BY GRADE
(1964 TO 1970)

YEAR	K	1-2	1	2	3	4	5	6	7	8	9	10	11	12	Sp	Total
						GRADE										
1964 to 1965	934	54	793	825	720	724	699	662	634	635	610	598	645	578	159	9,270
1965 to 1966	928	81	716	757	791	708	696	680	642	617	619	595	563	567	180	9,140
1966 to 1967	983	77	734	707	727	721	672	653	635	609	640	571	573	506	190	8,998
1967 to 1968	982	96	764	720	706	688	719	646	658	624	620	600	564	508	214	9,109
1968 to 1969	933	95	833	775	698	673	663	674	649	655	658	579	562	505	219	9,171
1969 to 1970	867	108	815	826	757	675	630	646	667	645	633	615	535	442	222	9,083

Source: Transition in the Plainfield Public Schools, Engelhardt and Engelhardt, 1970, p. 12.

EXHIBIT IV-3

PERCENTAGE DISTRIBUTION OF PLAINFIELD'S
PUBLIC SCHOOL ENROLLMENT
(1964 TO 1970)

YEAR	K	1-2	1	2	3	4	GRADE 5	6	7	8	9	10	11	12	Sp
1964 to 1965	10.1%	.6%	8.6%	8.9%	7.8%	7.8%	7.5%	7.1%	6.8%	6.9%	6.6%	6.5%	7.0%	6.2%	1.7%
1965 to 1966	10.2	.9	7.8	8.3	8.7	7.7	7.6	7.4	7.0	6.8	6.8	6.5	6.2	6.2	2.0
1966 to 1967	10.9	.9	8.2	7.9	8.1	8.0	7.5	7.3	7.1	6.8	7.1	6.3	6.4	5.6	2.1
1967 to 1968	10.8	1.1	8.4	7.8	7.7	7.6	7.9	7.1	7.2	6.9	6.8	6.6	6.1	5.8	2.3
1968 to 1969	10.2	1.0	9.1	8.5	7.6	7.3	7.2	7.3	7.1	7.1	7.2	6.3	6.1	5.5	2.4
1969 to 1970	9.5	1.2	9.0	9.1	8.3	7.4	6.9	7.1	7.3	7.1	7.0	6.8	5.9	4.9	2.4
Average percentage	10.2	.9	8.5	8.4	8.0	7.6	7.4	7.2	7.1	6.9	6.9	6.5	6.3	5.7	2.2

Source: See p. 125 of text, Exhibit IV-2.

entire school system over the last 10 school years. For the purposes of this study, however, it will be more meaningful to take each year's enrollment by grade and construct a table of percentages for each grade. Exhibit IV-3 displays these calculations. The last row contains the average percentage of total enrollment in each grade for the six-year period. This row shows a persistent erosion of the student population as it proceeds through the school system.

To ensure that different initial class sizes have not unduly influenced recognition of this trend, Exhibit IV-4 displays each individual cohort group as it advanced through 1965 to 1969.

This method permits allowance for any trend that may be limited to one particular calendar year. Exhibit IV-4 displays the percentage of students remaining in each successive pair of grades. The last row indicates that the year-to-year variation in the total number of students remaining is at most 2 percent; while in the last column on the right the average percentage of students remaining during each grade advance is for the most part decreasing at an increasing rate.

Three questions must be examined in order to explain this persistent drop in school population through the grades: 1) Is it common for schools in this area continually to lose a fraction of their enrollment? 2) Is it probable that there is an increasing out-migration of families with older children, an out-migration that increases with the length of the child's stay in the school? 3) Are the citizens of Plainfield removing their children from the schools as their length of stay increases?

ENROLLMENT CHANGES

In order to determine whether there is an area-wide pattern of declining enrollment with grade level, the enrollment change for each grade level in eight school districts near Plainfield has been calculated and is displayed in Exhibit IV-5.

Exhibit IV-6 compares the percentage distribution by grade for Plainfield with the averages of the other school districts. This shows that Plainfield's relatively higher proportion of children from kindergarten to fifth grade is declining at a higher rate than in the other districts. Both distributions are about the same during the fifth and sixth grades; thereafter, however, Plainfield continues to decline. In contrast, as a result of children from private schools coming into the other school districts the proportion of children entering the tenth grade is greater than that in the ninth grade. (See Exhibit IV-6 for a comparison of enrollments by grade for Plainfield and other districts.)

EXHIBIT IV-4

PERCENTAGE OF PUBLIC SCHOOL PUPILS REMAINING IN SCHOOL AFTER ADVANCING ONE YEAR

GRADES	1965	1966	1967	1968	1969	Average Percentage
1- 2	95.5%	98.7%	98.1%	101.4%	99.2%	98.6%
2- 3	95.9	96.0	99.9	96.9	97.7	97.3
3- 4	98.3	91.2	94.6	95.3	96.7	95.2
4- 5	96.1	94.9	99.7	96.4	93.6	96.1
5- 6	97.3	93.8	96.1	93.7	97.4	95.7
6- 7	97.0	93.4	100.7	100.5	99.0	97.9
7- 8	97.3	94.9	98.3	99.5	99.4	97.9
8- 9	97.5	103.7	101.8	105.4	96.6	101.0
9-10	97.5	92.2	93.8	93.4	93.5	94.1
10-11	94.1	96.3	98.7	93.7	92.4	95.0
11-12	87.9	89.9	88.7	89.5	78.6	86.9
Average year-to-year value	95.9	95.8	97.3	96.9	94.9	

Source: See p. 125 of text, Exhibit IV-2.

EXHIBIT IV-5

PUBLIC SCHOOL ENROLLMENT IN EIGHT
NEW JERSEY SCHOOL DISTRICTS
(1965 TO 1969 SCHOOL YEAR)

GRADE	Bayonne No.	%	Bloomfield No.	%	Hackensack No.	%	Linden No.	%	Average Percentage
K	698	7.6%	838	9.8%	411	6.7%	560	7.1%	8.6%
1	726	7.6	719	8.4	435	7.1	630	8.0	7.9
2	684	7.2	624	7.3	408	6.6	596	7.6	7.6
3	649	6.8	635	7.5	389	6.3	574	7.3	7.4
4	667	7.0	682	8.0	373	6.1	571	7.3	7.2
5	640	5.7	557	6.5	352	5.7	547	7.0	7.2
6	674	7.1	620	7.2	376	6.1	627	8.0	7.4
7	668	7.0	617	7.2	370	6.0	576	7.3	7.3
8	558	5.9	612	7.1	395	6.4	566	7.2	6.8
9	966	10.2	667	7.8	530	8.6	643	8.2	8.1
10	833	3.8	671	7.8	644	10.5	677	8.6	8.2
11	766	3.1	642	7.5	689	11.2	603	7.7	7.5
12	752	7.9	565	6.6	633	10.3	574	7.3	7.1
Special	219	2.3	113	1.3	143	2.3	111	1.4	1.5
Total number	9,500		8,562		6,148		7,855		
Total percentage		100.0%		100.0%		100.0%		100.0%	100.0%

Continued on p. 130.

EXHIBIT IV-5 (Continued)

PUBLIC SCHOOL ENROLLMENT IN EIGHT
NEW JERSEY SCHOOL DISTRICTS
(1965 TO 1969 SCHOOL YEAR)

GRADE	Orange		Rahway		Scotch Plains		Westfield		Average Percentage
	No.	%	No.	%	No.	%	No.	%	
K	656	13.9%	486	8.5%	744	9.2%	579	6.4%	8.6%
1	412	8.7	452	7.9	638	7.9	678	7.4	7.9
2	405	8.6	467	8.1	641	7.9	706	7.7	7.6
3	393	8.3	417	7.3	670	8.3	664	7.3	7.4
4	371	7.8	391	6.8	614	7.6	662	7.3	7.2
5	367	7.8	422	7.4	639	7.9	750	8.2	7.2
6	358	7.6	421	7.3	620	7.6	781	8.6	7.4
7	342	7.2	435	7.6	668	8.2	704	7.7	7.3
8	282	6.0	407	7.1	581	7.2	703	7.7	6.8
9	302	6.4	441	7.7	600	7.4	772	8.5	8.1
10	271	5.7	476	8.3	588	7.2	820	9.0	8.2
11	201	4.3	442	7.7	548	6.8	629	6.9	7.5
12	248	5.2	385	6.7	520	6.4	614	6.7	7.1
Special	119	2.5	96	1.7	47	.6	56	.6	1.5
Total number	4,727		5,738		8,118		9,118		
Total percentage		100.0%		100.0%		100.0%		100.0%	100.0%

Source: Annual Report, New Jersey Department of Education.

EXHIBIT IV-6

PERCENTAGE COMPARISON OF PLAINFIELD'S PUBLIC
SCHOOL ENFOLLMENT WITH OTHER NEW JERSEY
SCHOOL DISTRICTS

SCHOOL DISTRICT	K	1	2	3	4	GRADE 5	6	7	8	9	10	11	12
Plainfield	10.2%	8.5%	8.4%	8.0%	7.6%	7.4%	7.2%	7.1%	6.9%	6.9%	6.5%	6.3%	5.7%
Other	8.3	7.9	7.6	7.4	7.2	7.2	7.4	7.3	6.8	8.1	8.2	7.5	7.1

Source: Plainfield figures are from Exhibit IV-3. "Other" figures are from Exhibit IV-5.

SELECTIVE OUT-MIGRATION

The second possible reason for a declining school population is a selective out-migration of families with children in school, but this determination cannot be conclusive. Estimates of the population change in Plainfield by the State Department of Economic Development show that the population has increased since the last census. Although the family size and age distribution of those who have left Plainfield are not known, findings concerning the newcomers to the city show them to be predominantly families with children (Chapter I). One would therefore expect a slight increase in the school population rather than a decline.

Exhibit IV-7 displays the movements of the students and their families as indicated by school transfers, which average about 3,000 per year. In addition, for any one year there may be over 400 more students leaving the system than entering it.

Is there a selective out-migration that increases with time in school? A 5 percent random sampling of the outgoing transfers suggests not. Exhibit IV-8 displays two sets of information: column 1 shows the percentage distribution by grade of students transferring out of the school district for the 1969-1970 school year. This column is not corrected for the declining number of students in each grade, however. To allow for this correction index column 2 was constructed by finding for each grade the ratio of the percentage of students leaving to the percentage of students enrolled in that grade. If a condition of selective out-migration by grade exists, this index should increase in value from kindergarten to twelfth grade. Column 2 shows this not to be the case; rather, relatively large losses are found at three places—the second grade, the seventh grade and the twelfth grade.

EXHIBIT IV-7

STUDENT TRANSFERS

SCHOOL YEAR	Number of Students Leaving School District	Number of Students Moving Within School District	Number of Students Moving Into School District
1965 to 1966	1,379	727	967
1966 to 1967	963	665	1,291
1967 to 1968	902	605	1,272
1968 to 1969	1,200	615	1,193
1969 to 1970	1,119	709	1,273

Source: Attendance Office, Annual Reports, Plainfield Board of Education.

The failure of this explanation to give a satisfactory reason for the decline leaves one alternative; that is, that parents have an increasing tendency to remove their children from school as their stay in the system increases with time.

PRIVATE SCHOOLS

There exists one other factor affecting public school enrollment. A recent report prepared for the board of education estimates that 2,000 mostly white Plainfield children attend private and parochial schools.[1] However, St. Mary's Elementary School may discontinue service in the near future, and, potentially, 600 pupils would be added to the public school system.

The opinion (based upon birth records) has been expressed[2] that school enrollment will gradually decline. Our evidence suggests that this may be overly optimistic. Rather, there are three possible sources of pupils that will add to those born in this city—in-migration of new pupils, a return to the system of those children who are enrolled in other school systems (this is increasingly likely in view of the financial

EXHIBIT IV-8

DISTRIBUTION OF OUTGOING STUDENT TRANSFERS BY GRADE

GRADE	Percentage of a 5% Random Sample Leaving School System of Plainfield*	Index of Outgoing Students Correcting for Differing Sized Grades**
K	8.8%	.86
1	5.9	.69
2	13.1	1.56
3	10.2	1.30
4	5.9	.78
5	2.9	.39
6	5.9	.82
7	8.8	1.22
8	10.2	1.49
9	5.9	.85
10	7.3	1.12
11	7.3	1.16
12	7.3	1.28

Source: Plainfield Study, 1970.

*Percentage leaving school by grade $= \dfrac{\text{Number of students in sample leaving school from grade x}}{\text{Total number of students leaving school in the sample}}$

**Index of outgoing students corrected for grade size $= \dfrac{\text{Percentage leaving school from grade x}}{\text{Percentage of students enrolled in grade x}}$

problems of the parochial schools) and the greater retention of Plainfield's pupils as a result of the decreasing economic ability of Plainfield's school-involved population.

STUDENT POPULATION CHARACTERISTICS

Total enrollment in all schools for the 1970-1971 school year is 9,341;
4,119 students are enrolled in kindergarten through fourth grade;
1,269 are enrolled in fifth and sixth grade; 2,002 are in junior high
school; 251 are enrolled in special education programs (kindergarten
through twelfth grade); and 1,700 students are enrolled in the high
school.

The racial distribution of the school population at this time is: 68.8
percent are black, 28.1 percent are white and 3.1 percent are other. The
3.1 percent includes 2.7 percent of children who are from Spanish-
speaking homes. Fifty percent of the 253 children of Spanish origin are
enrolled in kindergarten through third grade.

The Spanish population is a recent addition to the city of Plainfield
and has considerable implications for the public school system. For
example, specific need has been expressed for additional bilingual
assistance. While the schools do have some assistance in the area now,
an increasing population will require additional help. Exhibit IV-9
shows racial distribution by grade. The history of bilingual programs
illustrates the shortcomings of depending on volunteers. When there
were relatively few children who had difficulties with the English

EXHIBIT IV-9

RACIAL DISTRIBUTION BY GRADE LEVEL

GRADES	Black	Percent of Total	Spanish	Percent of Total	Other	Percent of Total
K - 4	2,875	44.9%	141	55.8%	1,103	41.4%
5 - 6	928	14.4	20	7.9	321	12.0
7 - 9	1,447	22.5	49	19.4	506	18.9
10 - 12	972	15.1	32	12.6	696	26.2
Special education (elementary)	157	2.4	11	4.3	36	1.4
Special education (jr. high)	20	.3	0	0.0	0	0.0
Special education (sr. high)	25	.4	0	0.0	2	0.1
Total	6,424	100.0%	253	100.0%	2,664	100.0%

Source: Plainfield Board of Education.

language, a system of volunteer bilingual teacher's aides proved effective. However, too many children now need this kind of help, and language assistance must be institutionalized, its costs made specific.

SOCIOECONOMIC CHARACTERISTICS OF THE STUDENT POPULATION

An examination of all the public schools in Plainfield reveals that many of the students come from low- to middle-income families. Of enrollment in the 14 elementary and junior high schools, students from six were from low-income families with a tendency towards the welfare level[3]; principals from the schools reported that most of their students come from low-middle income families.

None of the principals indicated that their schools served an upper-middle-class population. A number of the principals said that many of the children in their schools come from homes that have both domestic and economic problems; these problems are frequently reflected in the children. The cultural inheritance of the different minority groups frequently places such children on a different footing from the dominant white culture.

The implications for the school are many. In some situations the burdens affect the youngsters' learning; in other situations the problems are displayed through poor behavior. The school is the stage on which the realities of our problems are shown.

Exhibit IV-10 identifies the changing composition of the student body. From 1963 to 1970 the elementary grades have changed from 43 percent black to 72 percent black. For the twelfth grade a similar pattern exists. Twenty-three percent of students who were in twelfth

EXHIBIT IV-10

PERCENTAGE DISTRIBUTION OF BLACK
CHILDREN IN THE PLAINFIELD
SCHOOL SYSTEM

GRADE	YEAR							
	1963	1964	1965	1966	1967	1968	1969	1970
1 - 6	43.6%	47.3%	50.8%	55.4%	60.3%	64.7%	68.6%	72.5%
7	37.1	39.7	45.2	44.9	54.7	62.2	72.7	73.4
8	36.1	38.1	42.6	49.3	49.2	56.8	65.8	75.4
9	28.9	37.7	39.6	43.0	47.4	50.6	59.8	67.9
10	30.5	30.3	37.9	39.9	46.3	50.1	59.9	61.8
11	27.9	31.2	30.7	37.2	42.4	47.2	48.8	57.3
12	23.4	26.3	31.8	29.1	38.4	38.6	45.6	50.5

Source: Attendance Reports, Plainfield School System.

grade in 1963 were black; in 1970, 50 percent of twelfth-graders were black.

This exhibit reveals another pattern which is all too similar to that found in other "mixed" school systems: not only has the absolute number of white non-Spanish-speaking students decreased sharply over the last eight years, but such students also are concentrated in the higher grades. About 25.9 percent of the non-Spanish-speaking whites are in tenth grade or above, as compared with 12.7 percent of the Spanish-speaking and 15.1 percent of the blacks. There is some indication that many of Plainfield's white parents are sending their children to private schools.

The very concept that equal education must be integrated education describes a state of affairs beyond the present delivery capacity of Plainfield. To the degree that this concept follows the functional reality, i.e., that integrated education really is required for minority groups to feel part of the overall scheme of things, and to meet their educational goals, Plainfield's educational capacity must suffer. In turn, the skew in racial distribution undoubtedly has a substantial effect on the characteristics of newcomers to the community.

How has this change in composition of the student body affected the learning disposition as measured by standardized tests? Educational tests and measurements are far from adequately developed. Their results should be viewed at best as giving insight into changes over time rather than absolute results. But even based on this type of analysis there has been a significant decline. The third grade students of 1965 were at the 104 level on the Kullman Anderson Measure of Academic Potential. By 1970 the equivalent group was under the 100 mark that is the national norm.

Even more striking, however, has been the response of the students to achievement tests. There has been a decided decline both by year and grade level. Based on the Iowa Tests of Basic Skills the performance of Plainfield's students is decidedly under the national norms. There is more of a decline in measured performance than in measured potential. The gap indicates the need for even more effort in the school system—and the community cannot afford it. Unless there is outside support for the school system it will have to falter. Given the importance of this input, the newcomer to the "zone of emergence" will find his goal much less rewarding than he had hoped for; the rung in the ladder to upward mobility for his children broken.

Plainfield's student body probably will grow in number as a function of population shift. In addition, there is a potential latent demand for education within Plainfield which is implied by the large enrollment in private and parochial schools and the increasing loss of students by grade.

Plainfield has found itself a center of immigration from other overflowing northern New Jersey central cities, from the farms of the Carolinas and, within the last three years, from Puerto Rico. Plainfield has accepted and will most certainly continue to receive American citizens who have needs that cannot be met without greatly expanding the educational system.

PHYSICAL PLANT NEEDS

Of the 16 schools in the Plainfield system, two were constructed in the late nineteenth century, while the newest one was built in 1970. A number of the schools were constructed during the early 1920s with additions that were completed in later years. Exhibit IV-11 shows the year of construction for each of the schools.

NUMBER OF CLASSROOMS

The number of classrooms per school ranges from a low of eight in the Lincoln School to a high of 27 in the Evergreen School. The high

EXHIBIT IV-11

AGES OF PLAINFIELD'S SCHOOLS

SCHOOL	Year Built	Date of Addition
Elementary (K-4)		
Barton	1939	1953
Cedarbrook	1954	
Clinton	1949	
Cook	1939	1953
Evergreen	1916	1967
Jefferson	1916	1922
Stillman	1951	1963
Woodland	1957	
Elementary (5-6)		
Emerson	1916	1967
Washington	1908	1958
Kindergarten and Spanish education		
Bryant (K. & Sp. Ed.)	1885	
Lincoln (Sp. Ed.)	1895	
Junior high school		
Hubbard	1927	1957
Maxon	1929	1957
Old high school*	1904	1913, 1929
New high school	1970	

Source: Englehardt Report, op. cit.
*Not presently in use.

school is not included in this range. Exhibit IV-12 shows the number of classrooms per school. Based on a standard of 25 students per class, the exhibit also shows the actual number of students and capacity for each school. While adequate for the present number of students, there is a high probability that additional physical plants will be needed because of the demographic changes discussed earlier.

LUNCHROOM FACILITIES

Because the Plainfield system serves a preponderance of low-income children, it is likely that many of the youngsters need school lunch facilities. In many cases, both parents work, particularly parents of children at the elementary school level. For these children, along with those pupils who are bussed out of their neighborhood, lunch time presents difficulties.

Of the 14 schools, five have space that is specifically designated as an eating facility, while the remaining schools have either improvised a facility or send the youngsters home. Although schools which send their

EXHIBIT IV-12

COMPARISON OF CAPACITIES AND ENROLLMENTS OF PLAINFIELD'S SCHOOLS

SCHOOL	Number of Classrooms[a]	Capacity[b]	Enrollment 1970[c]
Elementary (K-4)			
Barlow	14	350	341
Cedarbrook	20	500	619
Clinton	14	350	427
Cook	27	675	669
Evergreen	21	525	545
Jefferson	23	575	512
Stillman	13	325	347
Woodland	18	450	422
Elementary (5-6)			
Emerson	30	750	787
Washington	23	575	679
Spanish Education			
Bryant (K & Spec.)	10	150 }	244
Lincoln	8	120 }	
Junior high school			
Hubbard	36	900	945
Maxon	42	1,050	1,057
New high school		2,000	1,700

[a] Englehardt Report.
[b] Based on 25 students per classroom.
[c] Board of education.

children home for lunch do not have bussed children, they still have the problem of children with working parents. Moreover, of the five schools that have a lunchroom facility, only three have the capacity to provide hot lunches. None of these three facilities is modern. The lack of school cafeterias means that Plainfield's schools have to overcome many problems in order to utilize the national hot lunch program.

PROGRAM NEEDS

REMEDIAL READING

Each elementary school has one remedial reading teacher; each junior high school has one full-time and one half-time teacher; the high school has one. Most of the students who use this service are about two to three years below grade level. In most schools the children attend remedial reading sessions three times a week with a group. One remedial reading teacher can handle 50 students with sessions lasting 20 minutes but meeting daily. Due to the large enrollment, the groups meet three times a week. At least four more remedial reading teachers are needed, particularly for the lower elementary grades.

PREVENTIVE PROGRAM

The one need mentioned by virtually everyone in the Plainfield school system is the development of a strong preventive program in the early elementary school grades. Such a program would be devoted to identifying and halting the development of learning handicaps. Its aim would be to insure that by the time the child leaves fourth grade his reading and comprehension are at that grade level. An example of a preventive measure already implemented by the Plainfield school system is the fluid one two program. This program offers a flexible curriculum for children in the early grades who are not prepared for all of the experiences that would confront them in the separate grades. Since this program seems to have worked well on an experimental basis, it would seem plausible to introduce it in all of the schools for kindergarten through fourth grade. At this time, only two of the eight schools do not have a fluid class.

Particular importance is placed on a low pupil-teacher ratio in the lower grades when a preventive program is to be implemented. A class with a maximum of 20 students, as compared with the present average of 26, would allow the teacher to become aware of learning problems during very early stages of development. We suggest a class size of 20 students, based on a conservative recommendation of 25 students per regular class (from the State Department of Education) and 15 students per fluid class.

SPANISH-SPEAKING CHILDREN

Of special consideration must be the newest arrivals to the population in Plainfield school system—the Spanish-speaking youngsters, whose need for individualized attention is great. This points to a possibly growing need for bilingual personnel, as indicated earlier in this chapter.

SPECIAL SERVICES

High on the list of priorities expressed by school administrators is the need to expand special services. Almost all principals agreed that a social worker would be invaluable in assisting many students who are troubled either by outside pressures or those within the school itself. While there are at present four social workers on the special services staff, they are overtaxed by students with severe learning disabilities. The staff is able to handle only the most needy youngsters. Two additional social workers free to visit the schools and circulate would greatly alleviate the problem. Also of high priority is the need for additional speech therapists, since the four therapists now on the staff can handle only the most severe speech problems.

Function. The department of special services handles children who are experiencing learning disabilities for a wide range of reasons, including emotional disturbances, visual and auditory impairment, perceptual impairment, mental retardation and physical handicaps. It is the responsibility of the special services professional staff to evaluate and classify children referred to it by regular school personnel. The major concern of the staff is to evaluate the child and place him in an atmosphere that will be most conductive to his development.

Staff. At present the staff of this division consists of two psychologists, two learning disability specialists, four full-time social workers, three secretaries and one part-time psychiatrist. Staff members work both on an individual basis and as part of the child study team.

Child Study Team. The child study team is a unit of the department of special services. When a youngster is referred to this unit, a team consisting of a social worker, physician, psychologist, learning disability specialist and frequently a school nurse will participate in an evaluation process. Other specialists may also be included, depending on the specific nature of the problem. It is the composite opinion of this group that will ultimately classify the child and recommend a course of action to meet his needs.

Increased Need for Service. There appears to be a great need for such services in the Plainfield school system. Since 1965 two social workers, one learning disability specialist, a part-time psychiatrist, two secretaries and four-fifths of a psychologist's time have been added to the staff. At the end of the 1969-1970 school year there was a backlog of approximately 300 references that had not been evaluated and classified.

Although the size of the staff has increased over the last five years, the number of children who are in need of services has increased disproportionately. This increase has been attributed to the changing population, teachers' increased awareness of learning problems and the development of the child study team.

Projected Expenditure. The rise in the projected expenditures for the department of special services for the 1971-1972 school year is based on an increase in staff size in addition to an 8.5 percent increment for salary inflation.

The inclusion of additional staff for this service is based on standards formulated by Dr. Ronidine Machie, former consultant to the United States Office of Education. Dr. Machie recommends that a public school district have one school psychologist for every 1,500 students, one social worker for every 2,000 students, one learning disability specialist for every 1,500 students and one speech therapist for every 100 students requiring service.

Based on the above description, the projected budget (Exhibit IV-13) includes staff sufficient to meet the minimum standards as of the 1971-1972 school year. They are as follows: six learning disability specialists, five social workers, six psychologists, five speech therapists and a consulting psychiatrist. It would appear that the school system presently meets the standards for the number of social workers and speech therapists. Nonetheless, among the most frequently expressed needs of school administrators was a social worker (preferably bilingual) who could assist some of the students who did not go through the department of special services. In addition, administrators felt that an increment to the speech therapy staff was necessary. Thus, projected costs for this additional staff is also included in the exhibit.

DRUG EDUCATION

Plainfield's youth, like young people throughout the nation, have been afflicted with problems of drug abuse. In September 1970 the Plainfield Board of Education implemented a drug education program as a part of the total educational process.

Staff and Function of Drug Education Program. The staff of this department is limited at present to a coordinator, a part-time secretary and a part-time volunteer. The department's goal is to develop a drug education curriculum for kindergarten through twelfth grade. At the present time, the major emphasis is on providing school staff and com-

EXHIBIT IV-13

PROJECTED BUDGET FOR SPECIAL SERVICES

SERVICE	1970 to 1971	1971 to 1972	SCHOOL YEAR 1972 to 1973	1973 to 1974	1974 to 1975
Learning disability specialists	$ 43,000	$ 86,000	$ 93,000	$101,000	$110,000
Social workers	49,000	64,000	70,000	76,000	82,000
Psychologists	45,000	88,000	95,000	103,000	112,000
Speech therapists	40,000	53,000	58,000	63,000	68,000
Consulting psychiatrist	5,000	7,000	8,000	8,000	9,000
Total	$182,000	$298,000	$324,000	$351,000	$381,000

Source: See p. 140 of text, Chapter IV Special Services Section.

munity residents with an educational program. The full curriculum is
to be developed by early 1971.

HEALTH PROGRAM

Very often youngsters have learning disabilities due to a medical
problem that may be unknown to them and their families, for example,
the child who has a reading problem because of a hearing loss or poor
vision. The increased number of poor families with school-age children
raises the priority of the school health program among the auxiliary
services provided by the public school system.

The health program in Plainfield has two major components: one em-
phasizes the general physical well-being of the student, while the
second stresses the special problem areas that require psychological
evaluation. The latter area is handled by the child study team.

Staff. The health staff of the Plainfield school system currently has
a total of six full-time registered teacher-nurses and one supervising
nurse to serve the 9,338 students enrolled in the system. The staff also
includes two part-time medical doctors and one dental inspector.

Service Provided. The primary service provided by the school health
staff is the maintenance of minimum health standards as stipulated
by the State Department of Health. Included among these are child-
hood immunizations. Although all children entering kindergarten must
be inoculated, it has been found that many children do not meet this
requirement. As a result, approximately five years ago the nursing
staff established an immunization clinic with vaccine provided by the
Plainfield Division of Health.

The role of the school nursing staff encompasses a great deal more,
however. The nurses conduct an eye-screening program annually for
kindergarten and grades 1, 3, 5, 7, 9 and 11; during the 1969-1970 school
year 4,900 eye examinations were completed. They also perform an
auditory-screening examination for grades 1, 4, 7 and 11, and a tuber-
culosis test on all students and school staff.

Each year children in kindergarten and grades 4, 8 and 11 receive a
physical examination in addition to a dental inspection. If a problem is
detected, the school nurse will notify the parent with a recommendation
that the youngster have a more comprehensive examination.

Needs. Although the size of the school population has remained
stable over the last ten years, the current student body is more in need
of school health services than its predecessors. An enlarged nursing
staff could assist in this problem area. Among the major problems experienced by the nursing staff are the follow-up procedures when a
youngster is found to have a physical problem. Since households of the
affected children either do not have telephones or have parents who are

EXHIBIT IV-14

HEALTH BUDGET AS RELATED TO SCHOOL ENROLLMENT

	SCHOOL YEAR					
	1965 to 1966	1966 to 1967	1967 to 1968	1968 to 1969	1969 to 1970	1970 to 1971
Enrollment	9,140	8,998	9,109	9,171	9,083	9,338
Expenditures (in thousands of dollars)	$78,000	$85,000	$95,000	$107,000	$114,000	$129,000
Health expenditures per pupil	$ 8.5	$ 9.4	$ 10.4	$ 11.7	$ 12.6	$ 13.7
Percentage change of health budget (per pupil)	—	10.6%	10.6%	12.5%	7.6%	8.7%

Source: Budget Statements, Board of Education.

EXHIBIT IV-15

PROJECTED EXPENDITURES OF THE HEALTH DEPARTMENT

EXPENDITURE	Appropriations 1970 to 1971	Percentage Change	SCHOOL YEAR			
			1971 to 1972	1972 to 1973	1973 to 1974	1974 to 1975
Staff*	$104,000	8.2%	$149,000	$161,000	$174,000	$189,000
Materials	25,000	10.0	28,000	30,000	33,000	36,000

Source: Plainfield Study, 1970.
*With three new staff members included in 1971.

employed during school hours, the nurses often experience difficulty making contact with a member of the family. Unfortunately, due to lack of time and limited staff, home visits are very rare. Five hundred and forty notices were sent home during the 1969-1970 year after the screening examination, but only 232 parents acknowledged receiving them.

At the present time there is one nurse for each 1,300 students. This ratio makes if difficult to meet the needs of the youngsters under the best of circumstances, and Plainfield's children require more than an average amount of attention. Based on the state standard of one school nurse per 900 children, it will be necessary to add three nurses to the staff while assuming that the population will remain constant through 1975.

Expenditures. Exhibit IV-14 displays the cost of running the health program from 1965 through an estimate of the 1970-1971 school year. When this value is corrected for changes in enrollment, it shows a gradual increase in the money spent per child. As the yearly percentage change shows, however, this increase merely accounts for the prevailing inflation. Exhibit IV-15 shows the projected budget with a nonrecurring addition of three nurses in the 1971-1972 school year.

THE BOARD OF EDUCATION

This section will introduce the reader to the city's largest single expenditure unit—the school system.

The format of the analysis has been determined by the legislation which established, among other things, the budgetary framework of the different classes of school districts. The study opens with a descriptive paragraph for each major department in the budget, followed by an analysis of the major expenditure item and a concluding statement.

Following the pattern of the previous part of this chapter, we will conclude with a comparative analysis of the Plainfield school system with eight other northern New Jersey districts.

DESCRIPTION OF BUDGET CATEGORIES

The board of education maintains the school district by means of 14 categories of expenditure. These are shown in Exhibits IV-16 and IV-17. The initial concern is twofold: first to describe briefly the category and then, based upon the values shown in Exhibit IV-16, to determine the rank of each category. This will allow concentration of the analysis on the more sizable items.

EXHIBIT IV-16

EXPENDITURES OF THE PLAINFIELD
SCHOOL DISTRICT

EXPENDITURE	SCHOOL YEAR						
	1964 to 1965	1965 to 1966	1966 to 1967	1967 to 1968	1968 to 1969	1969 to 1970*	1970 to 1971*
Administration	$ 160	$ 165	$ 185	$ 228	$ 253	$ 258	$ 384
Instruction	3,684	4,003	4,368	4,880	5,399	6,139	6,882
Attendance & child services	16	17	17	38	42	13	40
Health services	70	76	84	95	107	114	128
Pupil transportation	63	82	96	203	199	223	252
Operation	471	503	537	590	654	746	968
Maintenance	207	268	283	250	257	303	331
Fixed charges	121	120	148	215	231	280	432
Student body activities	40	40	44	46	58	54	62
Community services	11	11	13	14	20	21	20
Capital outlay	30	30	82	73	84	131	140
Adult school	–	–	–	26	39	48	54
Evening school foreign-born	5	4	6	5	7	7	8
Other	2	26	242	52	91	172	111
Total	$4,880	$5,345	$6,105	$6,715	$7,441	$8,509	$9,812

Source: Budget Statements of the Plainfield Board of Education.
Note: Expenditure amounts are in thousands of dollars.
*Approximation.

EXHIBIT IV-17

ANNUAL PERCENTAGE DISTRIBUTION OF EXPENDITURES
OF THE PLAINFIELD SCHOOL DISTRICT

EXPENDITURE	SCHOOL YEAR						
	1964 to 1965	1965 to 1966	1966 to 1967	1967 to 1968	1968 to 1969	1969 to 1970	1970 to 1971
Administration	3.3%	3.1%	3.0%	3.4%	3.4%	3.0%	3.9%
Instruction	75.5	74.9	71.5	72.7	72.6	72.1	70.1
Attendance	.3	.3	.3	.6	.6	.1	.4
Health	1.4	1.4	1.4	1.4	1.4	1.3	1.3
Transportation	1.2	1.5	1.6	3.0	2.7	2.6	2.6
Operation	9.7	9.4	8.8	8.8	8.8	8.8	9.9
Maintenance	4.2	5.0	4.6	3.7	3.5	3.6	3.4
Fixed charges	2.5	2.2	2.4	3.2	3.1	3.3	4.4
Student body	.8	.7	.7	.7	.8	.6	.6
Community	.2	.2	.2	.2	.3	.2	.2
Capital	.6	.6	1.3	1.1	1.1	1.5	1.4
Adult school	—	—	—	.4	.5	.6	.6
Evening school	.1	.1	.1	.1	.1	.1	.1
Other	—*	.5	3.9	.8	1.2	2.0	1.1
Total	100.0%	100.0%	100.0%	100.0%	100.0%	100.0%	100.0%

Source: Budget Statements of the Plainfield Board of Education.

*Less than .1 percent.

ADMINISTRATION

The administration category contains funding for the superintendent's office, the business office and the board of education facilities. Services by such professionals as attorneys and architects, which are not continually maintained within the system, are funded under this category.

Administration has consistently accounted for approximately 4 percent of overall expenditures, placing it fourth in importance in terms of amount spent. Total expenditures have been increasing at a rate of over 16 percent a year, which makes it the second fastest growing item in the budget.

INSTRUCTION

The instructional category is and has been the largest expenditure item in the budget. Under this heading are not only the teachers, their supervisors and principals, but also the supplies and training devices needed for teaching and the improvement of teaching techniques.

As expected, this item is the highest cost category, involving over 70 percent of the expenditures each year and increasing in dollar volume by about 10 percent a year.

ATTENDANCE AND HEALTH SERVICES

The combined categories of attendance and health services account for less than 2 percent of the budget in the time period under analysis. Both, however, are significant programs. First, the attendance officer and his clerical staff maintain the attendance records. This is both a legal requirement and an important information source for determining future needs. The second element, health service, funds periodic medical and dental examinations. Costs for these services have declined slightly relative to those other categories of the budget, but have increased in actual dollars spent.

PUPIL TRANSPORTATION

Transportation services presently account for about 3 percent of the budget. These funds maintain and operate board-of-education-owned buses and out-of-city contract services for special education pupils. The large increase in this item during the 1967-1968 school year was caused by the increased number of students transported to private and parochial schools.

OPERATION

Throughout the period under examination operational expenditures have been the second highest expenditure, accounting for about 10 percent of the budget each year. This category funds the services of custodians, watchmen and the security force. Besides the supplies needed to continue the former services, the heat, electricity and other utilities are included. This item is increasing at an average of 13 percent per year.

MAINTENANCE

Maintenance expenditures have consistently been the fifth highest item, averaging over 4 percent of the budget. These funds allow a crew of mechanics to maintain continually the property of the board of education on both a planned and emergency basis. There are considerable changes in this item over time; however the average yearly increase is about 11 percent from each preceding year.

FIXED CHARGES

The category of fixed charges includes contributions to social security and state pension programs, insurance for both property, employees' health and workmen's compensation programs, and tuition for district students enrolled in special classes outside of the city.

An average increase of 25 percent per year has moved the category from fifth most important in the 1964-1965 school year to the fourth highest in the 1970-1971 appropriations, with 4 percent of current budget funds.

ANALYSIS OF REMAINING EXPENDITURE CATEGORIES

The remaining categories account for under 5 percent of the budget. None has changed enough to make it likely that it will affect the overall budget.

The first of these categories is student body activities. Funds in this category support interscholastic and intramural athletic programs. The category shows a decline in relative expenditures from 0.8 percent in the 1964-1965 year to .06 percent of the appropriations for the 1970-1971 school year.

The second category, community services, provides for the public use of board of education property by groups such as the municipal recreation commission, PTA and so forth. This service has been allotted

EXHIBIT IV-18

PERCENTAGE CHANGES IN THE FIVE HIGHEST
EXPENDITURE ITEMS OVER TIME

EXPENDITURE	SCHOOL YEAR					Average Percentage Change
	1964-65 to 1965-66	1965-66 to 1966-67	1966-67 to 1967-68	1967-68 to 1968-69	1968-69 to 1969-70	1969-70 to 1970-71
Administration	3.1%	12.1%	23.2%	11.0%	2.0%	48.8%	16.6%
Instruction	8.7	9.1	11.7	10.6	13.7	12.1	11.0
Operation	6.8	6.8	9.9	10.8	14.1	29.8	13.0
Fixed charges	0.0	23.3	45.3	7.4	21.2	54.3	25.1
Maintenance	29.4	5.7	-11.7	2.8	17.9	9.2	8.9

Source: Budget Statements of the Plainfield Board of Education.

approximately 2 percent of the budget each year.

The third category is capital outlay. This fund provides for specific projects such as building, remodelling and purchasing new types of instructional equipment. For the seven school years under consideration, capital outlay has averaged a little over 1 percent of the budget and is not projected to change significantly in the near future.

The final category involves two educational programs with a broader scope of community interest. The adult school, offering basic education, vocational training and retraining, commenced with the 1967-1968 school year. This program has been growing modestly since its inception and its funding is expected to increase in the next five years to close to 1 percent of the total budget.

The evening school for the foreign born is a traditional program which has operated for over 50 years. With its estimated enrollment of 200 persons, the program requires about 1 percent of the budget and has remained at this level throughout the seven school years analyzed.

* * *

The results of this analysis demonstrate that five of the 14 categories account for over 90 percent of the school budget each year. The five categories displayed in Exhibit IV-18 will be described further to determine how the funds are spent and how these patterns are changing over time.

MAJOR EXPENDITURES

Administration

Earlier, administration has been shown to account for about 4 percent of the budget. Exhibits IV-18 and IV-19 reveal that salaries and wages to the permanent personnel are by far the most important item, presently holding over 80 percent of the expenditures for the category. The large increase in salaries requested for 1971 is due to a proposed increase in new personnel, an increase whose duplication is not anticipated in the near future.

Exhibit IV-20 shows the yearly percentage change for salaries and compares it with the change in total administrative expenditures. Over the six pairs of years the two are similar, with about a 17 percent increase per year. This indicates the anchoring effect of salaries over the other two items; however, it also suggests the potential for increased expenditures based on results shown in Exhibit IV-21.

Assuming a slight growth in enrollment and additional needs for educational leadership, this category must be assumed to increase in a pattern similar to its past, exclusive of any large increase in administrative personnel.

EXHIBIT IV-19

ADMINISTRATIVE EXPENDITURES OF THE PLAINFIELD BOARD OF EDUCATION

					SCHOOL YEAR			
EXPENDITURE	1964 to 1965	1965 to 1966	1966 to 1967	1967 to 1968	1968 to 1969	1969 to 1970	1970 to 1971
Salaries	$123,000	$137,000	$158,000	$181,000	$196,000	$218,000	$313,000
Contracted services	19,000	9,000	7,000	18,000	23,000	11,000	29,000
Other	18,000	18,000	20,000	28,000	33,000	30,000	42,000
Total	$160,000	$164,000	$185,000	$227,000	$252,000	$259,000	$384,000

Source: Budget Statements, Plainfield Board of Education.

EXHIBIT IV-20

PERCENTAGE DISTRIBUTION OF ADMINISTRATIVE EXPENDITURES BY SCHOOL YEAR

					SCHOOL YEAR			
EXPENDITURE	1964 to 1965	1965 to 1966	1966 to 1967	1967 to 1968	1968 to 1969	1969 to 1970	1970 to 1971
Salaries	76.9%	83.5%	85.4%	79.7%	77.7%	84.2%	81.5%
Contracted services	11.9	5.5	3.8	7.9	9.1	4.2	7.6
Other	11.2	11.0	10.8	12.4	13.2	11.6	10.9
Total	100.0%	100.0%	100.0%	100.0%	100.0%	100.0%	100.0%

Source: Budget Statements, Plainfield Board of Education.

EXHIBIT IV-21

PERCENTAGE CHANGE IN ADMINISTRATIVE
EXPENDITURES OVER TIME

EXPENDITURE	SCHOOL YEAR						Average Change
	1964-65 to 1965-66	1965-66 to 1966-67	1966-67 to 1967-68	1967-68 to 1968-69	1968-69 to 1969-70	1969-70 to 1970-71	
Salaries	11.4%	15.3%	14.6%	8.3%	11.2%	43.6%	17.4%
Contracted services	-53.8	-30.9	157.1	27.8	-52.2	164.2	39.7
Other	0.0	11.3	40.8	17.8	-10.0	40.1	16.4
Total administrative expenditures	3.1	12.1	23.2	11.0	1.6	48.8	16.6

Source: Budget Statements, Plainfield Board of Education.

EXHIBIT IV-21a

INSTRUCTIONAL EXPENDITURES

EXPENDITURE	SCHOOL YEAR						
	1964 to 1965	1965 to 1966	1966 to 1967	1967 to 1968	1968 to 1969	1969 to 1970	1970 to 1971
Salaries							
Principals	$ 194	$ 205	$ 233	$ 254	$ 297	$ 358	$ 366
Supervisors	79	74	82	62	85	113	142
Teachers	2,900	3,171	3,474	3,893	4,241	4,711	4,978
Others	300	335	358	411	481	656	783
Textbooks	56	63	70	81	61	81	88
Library and A-V	26	28	31	38	49	56	59
Teaching supplies	92	94	94	96	105	112	119
Other expenses	33	33	45	45	80	53	134
Total	$3,681	$4,003	$4,387	$4,880	$5,399	$6,140	$6,669

Source: Budget Statements, Plainfield Board of Education.

Note: Expenditure amounts are in thousands of dollars.

Instruction

The instructional category funds the largest group of services, those rendered by the teaching staff and their immediate supervisors. Exhibits IV-21 through IV-24 show the subdivisions and their percentage changes throughout the seven-year period.

Most prominent is the size of the expenditures going directly to the teaching staff. Though the staff's salary dropped 5 percent in relative expenditures, it still accounts for 74 percent of the total. This 5 percent drop has been caused by the relative increase in the salaries of principals and other professional staff such as librarians, guidance counselors, psychologists, learning disability specialists and group social workers.

Contrasting the percentage changes of the salary items with that of the teaching supply and aids category, a much smaller and sporadic type of change in the expenditures of the latter is seen.

Demand for teaching supplies, library books and other materials may be increasing; however, with the bulk of the cost being due to the salaries for the staff of nearly 500, even fractional increases in salaries will far outweigh outlays for materials. It is personnel costs that will determine the future.

Operational Expenditures

The operating costs for a system using 16 physical plants entails a significant portion of the total budget. As has been seen previously, this portion is about 10 percent and is growing at a rate comparable to the other categories.

Exhibits IV-24 through IV-26 contain the subdivisions within this category. As in the previous case, salaries are the largest item, averaging about 69 percent of the yearly budget. The last several years of unrest has brought a need for a security force and additional custodial help; thus, there has been a functional increase in staff size, duplication of which is not anticipated in the future.

Thus, under the continuing existence of physical plant and security needs, the average percentage distribution reflected in Exhibit IV-25 should continue with growth in dollar value determined predominantly by requests for higher wages.

Fixed Charges

The fixed charges category is tied predominantly to personnel expenditures made in previous categories. Pension contributions are mandated by federal and state enactments and depend upon the salary levels and size of the staff. Insurance includes two items: first, health

EXHIBIT IV-22

PERCENTAGE DISTRIBUTION OF INSTRUCTIONAL
EXPENDITURES BY YEAR

EXPENDITURE	1964 to 1965	1965 to 1966	1966 to 1967	1967 to 1968	1968 to 1969	1969 to 1970	1970 to 1971
				SCHOOL YEAR			
Salaries							
Principals	5.3%	5.1%	5.3%	5.2%	5.5%	5.8%	5.5%
Supervisors	2.1	1.8	1.9	1.3	1.6	1.8	2.1
Teachers	78.9	79.2	79.2	79.8	78.6	76.8	74.8
Others	8.1	8.4	8.2	8.4	8.9	10.7	11.7
Textbooks	1.5	1.6	1.6	1.7	1.1	1.3	1.3
Library and A-V	.7	.7	.7	.8	.9	.9	.8
Teaching supplies	2.5	2.3	2.1	2.0	1.9	1.8	1.8
Other expenses	.9	0.9	1.0	.8	1.5	.9	2.0
Total	100.0%	100.0%	100.0%	100.0%	100.0%	100.0%	100.0%

Source: Budget Statements, Plainfield Board of Education.

EXHIBIT IV-23

PERCENTAGE CHANGE IN INSTRUCTIONAL
EXPENDITURES FROM YEAR TO YEAR

			SCHOOL YEAR			
EXPENDITURE	1964-65 to 1965-66	1965-66 to 1966-67	1966-67 to 1967-68	1967-68 to 1968-69	1968-69 to 1969-70	1969-70 to 1970-71	Average Change
Salaries							
Principals	5.7%	13.7%	9.0%	16.9%	20.5%	19.3%	14.0%
Supervisors	-6.3	10.8	-24.4	37.1	32.9	53.9	21.6
Teachers	9.3	9.6	12.1	8.9	11.1	8.2	11.4
Others	11.7	6.9	14.8	17.0	50.3	19.4	20.0
Textbooks	10.7	11.1	12.9	-12.3	32.8	8.6	10.6
Library and A-V	7.7	10.7	22.6	28.9	14.3	5.3	14.9
Teaching supplies	2.2	0.0	2.1	9.4	6.7	6.3	4.5
Other	0.0	36.3	0.0	77.7	-33.8	152.8	38.2
Annual total percentage change	8.7%	9.6%	11.2%	10.6%	13.7%	12.1%	

Source: Budget Statements, Plainfield Board of Education.

EXHIBIT IV -24

OPERATIONAL EXPENDITURES FOR THE PLAINFIELD
BOARD OF EDUCATION

EXPENDITURE				SCHOOL YEAR			
	1964 to 1965	1965 to 1966	1966 to 1967	1967 to 1968	1968 to 1969	1969 to 1970	1970 to 1971
Custodial services	$327,000	$348,000	$372,000	$417,000	$450,000	$565,000	$ 739,000
Heat	40,000	40,000	43,000	40,000	47,000	48,000	68,000
Utilities	85,000	91,000	94,000	143,000	156,000	149,000	194,000
Supplies	17,000	18,000	20,000	22,000	21,000	22,000	25,000
Other	2,000	6,000	8,000	7,000	30,000	9,000	10,000
Total	$471,000	$503,000	$537,000	$629,000	$704,000	$793,000	$1,036,000

Source: Budget Statements, Plainfield Board of Education.

EXHIBIT IV-25

PERCENTAGE DISTRIBUTION OF OPERATIONAL EXPENDITURES BY YEAR

EXPENDITURE				SCHOOL YEAR				
	1964 to 1965	1965 to 1966	1966 to 1967	1967 to 1968	1968 to 1969	1969 to 1970	1970 to 1971	Average Percentage Distribution
Custodial service	69.4%	69.2%	69.3%	66.3%	63.9%	71.2%	71.3%	69.0%
Heat	8.5	8.0	8.0	6.4	6.7	6.1	6.6	7.2
Utilities	18.1	18.1	17.5	22.7	22.2	18.8	18.7	19.4
Supplies	3.6	3.6	3.7	3.5	3.0	2.8	2.4	3.2
Other	.4	1.1	1.5	1.1	4.3	1.1	1.0	1.5
Total	100.0%	100.0%	100.0%	100.0%	100.0%	100.0%	100.0%	

Source: Budget Statements, Plainfield Board of Education.

EXHIBIT IV-26

PERCENTAGE CHANGE IN OPERATIONAL EXPENDITURE ITEMS, FROM SCHOOL YEAR TO SCHOOL YEAR

EXPENDITURE	SCHOOL YEAR						Average Change
	1964-65 to 1965-66	1965-66 to 1966-67	1966-67 to 1967-68	1967-68 to 1968-69	1968-69 to 1969-70	1969-70 to 1970-71	
Custodial service	6.4%	6.8%	12.1%	7.9%	25.6%	30.8%	14.9%
Heat	0.0	7.5	-7.0	17.5	2.1	41.7	9.9
Utilities	7.1	3.3	52.1	5.6	0.0	31.0	16.5
Supplies	5.9	11.1	10.0	0.0	0.0	13.6	6.8

Source: Budget Statements, Plainfield Board of Education.

EXHIBIT IV-27

FIXED CHARGES OF THE PLAINFIELD BOARD OF EDUCATION

EXPENDITURE	SCHOOL YEAR						
	1964 to 1965	1965 to 1966	1966 to 1967	1967 to 1968	1968 to 1969	1969 to 1970	1970 to 1971
Pensions	$ 80,000	$ 83,000	$107,000	$121,000	$137,000	$136,000	$152,000
Insurance	33,000	36,000	41,000	94,000	94,000	145,000	280,000
Tuition (Beadleston Act)	8,000	1,000	1,000	24,000	56,000	60,000	66,000
Total	$121,000	$120,000	$149,000	$239,000	$287,000	$341,000	$498,000

Source: Budget Statements, Plainfield Board of Education.

insurance granted to the teachers by the board of education; and second, general liability coverage on the building and grounds of the system. Tuition payments are substantially covered by the recently enacted Beadleston Act from which the special education needs of exceptional students will be provided through state refunds to the local school district.

Exhibits IV-27 through IV-29 show the pattern of increase for these expenditures. Pension and tuition costs are increasing at about the average inflation rate; however, three factors influenced the insurance category: first, the initial civil unrest of 1967; second, the addition of the new high school; third, the complete assumption of medical insurance payments by the city. These three factors augment the general inflation. No new responsibilities are anticipated; therefore, the percentage distribution of items for the 1970-1971 school year may be considered the base for projecting future expenditures.

Maintenance

The maintenance category presently is the fifth highest expenditure item, having fallen relative to administrative and fixed charges. Differing from the other categories, salaries to permanent personnel are not the largest item but are one of two important subdivisions—the other being contracted labor and equipment. Exhibits IV-30 through IV-32 show that these two items have accounted for 70 percent of the maintenance budget each year. The yearly changes in each item have been noticeably erratic. When averaged over the six successive time periods, the yearly changes have been remarkably similar to the average changes within the operations category.

The five major expenditure categories of the board of education have been described and analyzed in detail in order to find the reasons for rising costs. Two factors were examined throughout: first, an ever-present inflation which combines the price level increase within our regional economy with the very strong demands of government employees for high wages; and second, planned and unplanned responsibility increases brought about by changes in educational technology, plant expansion, civil unrest.

ANALYSIS OF EDUCATIONAL EXPENDITURES IN TERMS OF SERVICES AND GOODS

An earlier chapter in this volume showed that municipal government expended 70 percent of its average annual budget on services or

EXHIBIT IV-28

PERCENTAGE DISTRIBUTION OF FIXED CHARGES OVER TIME

EXPENDITURE	SCHOOL YEAR						
	1964 to 1965	1965 to 1966	1966 to 1967	1967 to 1968	1968 to 1969	1969 to 1970	1970 to 1971
Pensions	66.1%	69.2%	71.8%	50.6%	47.7%	39.9%	30.5%
Insurance	27.3	30.1	27.5	39.3	32.8	42.5	56.2
Tuition	6.6	0.7	0.7	10.1	19.5	17.6	13.3
Total	100.0%	100.0%	100.0%	100.0%	100.0%	100.0%	100.0%

Source: Budget Statements, Plainfield Board of Education.

EXHIBIT IV-29

PERCENTAGE CHANGE IN FIXED CHARGES EXPENDITURES

EXPENDITURE	SCHOOL YEAR						
	1964-65 to 1965-66	1965-66 to 1966-67	1966-67 to 1967-68	1967-68 to 1968-69	1968-69 to 1969-70	1969-70 to 1970-71	Average Change
Pensions	3.8%	28.9%	13.1%	13.2%	.0%	11.8%	12.0%
Insurance	9.1	13.9	129.3	0.0	54.3	93.1	50.1
Tuition	—*	—*	—*	133.3**	7.1	10.0	8.5***

Source: Budget Statements, Plainfield Board of Education.

*Calculated values not meaningful.

**Reflects Expansion of Tuition Program.

***Exclusive of Policy Change reflected in 1967-68 to 1968-69 percentage change.

EXHIBIT IV-30

MAINTENANCE EXPENDITURES OF THE PLAINFIELD
BOARD OF EDUCATION

EXPENDITURE	1964 to 1965	1965 to 1966	1966 to 1967	SCHOOL YEAR 1967 to 1968	1968 to 1969	1969 to 1970	1970 to 1971
Salaries	$ 65,000	$ 83,000	$ 90,000	$ 85,000	$ 93,000	$ 93,000	$110,000
Contracted services	75,000	107,000	119,000	93,000	90,000	105,000	117,000
Replacement of equipment	24,000	21,000	33,000	33,000	27,000	55,000	45,000
Other	42,000	56,000	41,000	39,000	45,000	51,000	57,000
Total	$206,000	$267,000	$283,000	$250,000	$255,000	$304,000	$329,000

Source: Budget Statements, Plainfield Board of Education.

EXHIBIT IV-31

PERCENTAGE DISTRIBUTION OF MAINTENANCE EXPENDITURES
BY SCHOOL YEAR

EXPENDITURE				SCHOOL YEAR			
	1964 to 1965	1965 to 1966	1966 to 1967	1967 to 1968	1968 to 1969	1969 to 1970	1970 to 1971
Salaries	31.6%	31.1%	31.8%	34.0%	36.5%	30.6%	33.4%
Contracted services	36.4	40.1	42.0	37.2	35.3	34.5	35.6
Replacement of equipment	11.7	7.9	11.7	13.2	10.6	18.1	13.7
Other	20.3	20.9	14.5	15.6	17.6	16.8	17.3
Total	100.0%	100.0%	100.0%	100.0%	100.0%	100.0%	100.0%

Source: Budget Statements, Plainfield Board of Education.

personnel items. This section will apply a similar analysis to the expenditures of the board of education.

Exhibits IV-33 and IV-34 show similar results—indicating the importance of personnel costs over all other items. Even though the salary item has declined slightly in relative value, it still accounts for over 75 percent of the budget.

Exhibit IV-35 indicates the number of persons grouped under each personnel heading. With this information and the expenditures for salaries for each category, the average salary for that category of personnel has been estimated. This is shown in Exhibit IV-36. Each category contains a set of occupational specialties. For example, the administrative category includes both the superintendent and his immediate staff and clerical personnel. Under instruction, the "others" category includes both clerical personnel used in the schools and professional personnel, such as learning specialists, guidance counselors and librarians. The average growth in salaries shown here does not permit an interpretation of what changes are taking place within a category such as administration, with its grouping of the supervisors, their immediate staff and clerical personnel.

Exhibit IV-37 lists each of the salary categories and compares their average change both yearly and over the seven school years studied. It shows that each category has kept up with the inflation as measured by the Consumer Price Index (CPI) of northern New Jersey—metropolitan area indicators. The last column shows how much more certain salary categories have changed than the CPI. The "others" category is 71 percent above the CPI. This, it must be remembered, encompasses a varied group of specialists whose numbers have increased 22 percent from 1964-1965 to 1970-1971.

The two most stable categories in terms of numbers of individuals are the principals and maintenance categories. They have both grown relative to the CPI by about 11 percent.

In this section the educational expenditures for the board of education have been presented. These expenditures are increasing at a rate exceeding the inflationary indicator. Further, as was shown for municipal expenditures, personnel costs are the largest item in the budget and are increasing at a higher rate than other expenditures.

THE PLAINFIELD SCHOOL SYSTEM AND OTHER NEW JERSEY SCHOOL SYSTEMS

The earlier part of this chapter has summarized Plainfield's school situation in terms of need and in terms of the costs of serving past and

EXHIBIT IV-32

PERCENTAGE CHANGE IN MAINTENANCE EXPENDITURES OVER TIME

EXPENDITURE	SCHOOL YEAR						Average Change
	1964-65 to 1965-66	1965-66 to 1966-67	1966-67 to 1967-68	1967-68 to 1968-69	1968-69 to 1969-70	1969-70 to 1970-71	
Salaries	27.6%	8.4%	5.6%	9.4%	0.0%	18.3%	9.6%
Contracted services	42.7	11.2	−21.8	3.2	16.7	11.4	10.6
Replacement of equipment	−12.5	57.1	0.0	−18.2	103.7	−18.2	18.7
Other	33.3	−26.8	− 4.9	15.4	13.3	11.8	7.0

Source: Budget Statements, Plainfield Board of Education.

EXHIBIT IV-33

SCHOOL DISTRICT PERSONNEL COSTS COMPARED WITH ALL OTHER SCHOOL DISTRICT EXPENDITURES

EXPENDITURE	SCHOOL YEAR						
	1964 to 1965	1965 to 1966	1966 to 1967	1967 to 1968	1968 to 1969	1969 to 1970	1970 to 1971
Salaries	$3,742	$4,353	$4,767	$5,303	$5,843	$6,714	$7,431
Other expenditures	1,138	992	1,338	1,412	1,598	1,795	2,381
Total	$4,880	$5,345	$6,105	$6,715	$7,441	$8,509	$9,812

Source: Budget Statements, Plainfield Board of Education.
Note: All expenditure amounts are in thousands of dollars.

EXHIBIT IV-34

ANNUAL PERCENTAGE DISTRIBUTION OF PERSONNEL AND OTHER EXPENDITURES OF THE BOARD OF EDUCATION

EXPENDITURE	SCHOOL YEAR						
	1964 to 1965	1965 to 1966	1966 to 1967	1967 to 1968	1968 to 1969	1969 to 1970	1970 to 1971
Salaries	76.7%	81.4%	78.1%	78.9%	78.5%	78.9%	75.7%
Other	23.3	19.6	21.9	21.1	21.5	21.1	24.3
Total	100.0%	100.0%	100.0%	100.0%	100.0%	100.0%	100.0%

Source: See p. 167 of text.

EXHIBIT IV-35

AVERAGE ANNUAL NUMBER OF SALARIED AND WAGE PERSONNEL, PLAINFIELD BOARD OF EDUCATION

EXPENDITURE	SCHOOL YEAR						
	1964 to 1965	1965 to 1966	1966 to 1967	1967 to 1968	1968 to 1969	1969 to 1970	1970 to 1971
Administration No. of salaried personnel	15	16	17	17	17	18	27
Instruction							
Teachers	411	425	433	432	444	450	469
Principals	17	17	19	19	20	20	21
Supervisors	8	7	8	6	8	9	11
Other	55	57	59	60	60	65	67
Operations	57	57	57	57	62	70	90
Maintenance	9	10	10	9	10	10	10

Source: Periodic Reports from the Plainfield Board of Education.

EXHIBIT IV-36

AVERAGE ANNUAL SALARY IN SELECTED EXPENDITURE
CATEGORIES OF THE BOARD OF EDUCATION

CATEGORY	1964 to 1965	1965 to 1966	1966 to 1967	SCHOOL YEAR 1967 to 1968	1968 to 1969	1969 to 1970	1970 to 1971
Administration	$ 8,200	$ 8,600	$ 9,300	$10,600	$11,500	$12,200	$11,600
Instruction							
Teachers	7,100	7,500	8,000	9,000	9,600	10,500	10,600
Principals	11,400	12,000	12,300	13,400	14,800	17,900	17,400
Supervisors	9,800	10,500	10,300	10,300	10,600	12,600	15,800
Others	5,500	5,900	6,100	7,000	8,000	10,100	11,700
Operations	5,700	6,100	6,500	7,300	7,300	8,000	8,200
Maintenance	7,200	8,300	9,000	9,400	9,300	9,300	11,000

Source: Salary Reports, Board of Education.

present students. In this section Plainfield's educational expenditures are evaluated through comparisons with those of other northern New Jersey school districts. The analysis gives some insight into the fiscal burdens and efforts of the community.

A comparative analysis using summary figures must not, however, be construed as being an evaluator of quality. These figures will not indicate how well the various groups of instructional personnel are performing nor the cooperation any one of them receives from the other. It will not tell the quality of education that the different groups of students are receiving. At best, it will merely compare the external indicators with other school districts. For this comparative analysis six different indicators will be used: 1) percentage of population enrolled as day school pupils; 2) equalized school tax rate; 3) equalized valuation of all taxable property per pupil; 4) current expense cost per pupil; 5) teacher salary cost per pupil; and 6) number of professional staff members per 1,000 weighted pupils.

Nine New Jersey school districts with enrollments of over 6,000 pupils per year will be compared for the school years 1964-1965 to 1968-1969. In order to describe Plainfield's position within each distribution, the median and interquartile range will be displayed in addition to the statistics for the individual districts. The use of these statistics allows correction for extreme values by indicating the values of the interquartile range, where the middle 50 percent of the cases lie; the median gives us the score of the school district which is in the middle of this distribution.

INTERPRETATION OF EXHIBITS

In order to provide some idea of the age characteristics of pupils from each municipality as related to the school enrollment, Exhibit IV-38 displays the percentage of each municipality's population that is enrolled in the public school system. This exhibit shows the extremes on one end to be Bayonne and Orange, with a relatively small proportion of school children, and on the other end, Scotch Plains and Westfield with twice Bayonne's enrollment. Plainfield and the four remaining districts lie between these extremes.

Exhibit IV-39 displays the equalized school tax rate for a six-year period. In each case, Plainfield is in the highest quartile of tax rates, indicating the citizen's tax effort for educational services.

Exhibit IV-40, the equalized valuation of taxable property per pupil, allows comparison of taxable capacity. In each case Plainfield is in the lowest quartile. This means that Plainfield has one of the highest expenditures for education while its ability to pay for it is one of the

EXHIBIT IV-37

PERCENTAGE CHANGE IN AVERAGE SCHOOL SALARIES
FROM 1964-65 TO 1970-71

CATEGORY	(1) Average Yearly Percentage Change	(2) Total Percentage Change in Salaries 1964-65 to 1970-71	(3) Total Percentage Change of CPI 1965 to 1970	(4) Difference Between Salary and Inflational Changes Measured by CPI
Administration	6.9%	41.5%	26.2%	15.3%
Instruction				
Teachers	8.2	49.3	26.2	23.1
Principals	8.8	52.6	26.2	26.4
Supervisors	10.2	61.2	26.2	35.0
Others	18.8	112.7	26.2	86.5
Operation	7.3	43.9	26.2	17.7
Maintenance	8.8	52.8	26.2	26.6

Source: Plainfield Study, 1970.

EXHIBIT IV 38

ESTIMATED PERCENTAGE OF POPULATION ENROLLED IN PUBLIC SCHOOLS FOR SELECTED NEW JERSEY MUNICIPALITIES

MUNICIPALITY	(1) Population Estimate: 1960	(2) Enrollment: 1968 to 1969	Enrollment as Percentage of Population
Bayonne	74,215	9,500	12.8%
Bloomfield	51,867	8,562	16.5
Hackensack	30,521	6,145	20.1
Linden	39,931	7,855	19.7
Orange	35,789	4,727	13.2
Rahway	27,699	5,738	20.7
Scotch Plains			
(& Fanwood)	26,454	8,118	30.7
Westfield	31,447	9,118	28.9
Plainfield	45,330	9,083	20.0

Source: Column (1) was taken from Legislative Manual Study New Jersey — J. Gorbbins, 1970. Column (2) is from Annual Report of the Commissioner of Education.

EXHIBIT IV-39

EQUALIZED SCHOOL TAX RATE FOR SELECTED NEW JERSEY MUNICIPALITIES

MUNICIPALITY	YEAR					
	1965	1966	1967	1968	1969	1970*
Bayonne	1.15%	1.19%	1.29%	1.58%	1.57%	1.77%
Bloomfield	1.56	1.54	1.61	1.59	1.71	1.90
Hackensack	1.17	1.12	1.16	1.46	1.41	1.52
Linden	.85	.77	.73	.86	.89	1.04
Orange	1.72	1.69	1.87	2.07	2.26	2.48
Rahway	1.45	1.39	1.34	1.61	1.73	1.92
Scotch Plains	1.91	1.89	2.02	2.43	2.78	2.40
Westfield	1.82	1.82	1.89	2.20	2.12	2.33
Plainfield	2.08	1.91	2.11	2.46	2.74	2.97
Median	1.56	1.54	1.61	1.61	1.73	1.92
Interquartile range	1.17-1.82	1.19-1.82	1.29-1.89	1.58-2.20	1.57-2.28	1.77-2.40

Source: N.J.E.A. Research Bulletin, "Basic Statistical Data of New Jersey School Districts."
*Estimated.

EXHIBIT IV-40

EQUALIZED VALUATION PER PUPIL FOR SELECTED
NEW JERSEY MUNICIPALITIES
(ROUNDED TO THE NEAREST THOUSAND DOLLARS)

MUNICIPALITY	SCHOOL YEAR					
	1964 to 1965	1965 to 1966	1966 to 1967	1967 to 1968	1968 to 1969	
Bayonne	$37	$38	$40	$36	$40	
Bloomfield	38	40	44	44	42	
Hackensack	59	60	64	71	71	
Linden	70	79	81	76	78	
Orange	33	35	36	34	34	
Rahway	32	35	34	35	36	
Scotch Plains	29	30	31	32	33	
Westfield	31	33	33	34	37	
Plainfield	27	29	30	30	30	
Median	33	35	36	35	37	
Interquartile range	$31-38	$33-40	$33-44	$34-44	$34-42	

Source: N.J.E.A. Research Bulletin, "Basic Statistical Data of New Jersey School Districts."

lowest. Exhibit IV-41 shows that Plainfield has been maintaining, with a slight increase, its position within the interquartile range in per pupil expenditure. There is a range of about 300 per pupil each year between the highest and lowest school district in the average amount spent on each pupil. Thus, the extreme effort made by the taxpayers only allows Plainfield to maintain its middle position in the distribution of school districts.

Exhibit IV-42 shows the effort to maintain a qualified professional staff. Teachers' salaries measured in dollars expended per pupil show a pattern similar to expenditures per pupil; that is, that the district has always been within the interquartile range and has moved from a bit below the median at the beginning of the time period to a bit above the median in the last period.

Exhibit IV-43 indicates the number of professional staff members per 1,000 weighted pupils. Hackensack has remained at the top of the list throughout the period. Plainfield has been very close to the median.

In a comparison with nine school districts with similar enrollments, Plainfield's citizens are making the highest tax effort to maintain schools while having one of the smallest tax bases. This effort, however, has merely maintained the benefit indicators—expenditures per pupil, teacher salaries and teacher-pupil ratio—at about the median of each of the distributions, indicating that any slackening of this tax effort would plunge Plainfield into the lower levels of performance. Yet, despite the level of expenditures in Plainfield, the gap between student capacities and accomplishments continues to widen. And the community cannot provide much more support.

The analysis in this chapter of board of education expenditures has revealed a situation similar to that shown in the chapter on municipal government. In both cases, expenditures, after correcting for new services, are increasing at a rate above the CPI, and personnel items are by far the major portion of each budget.

FOOTNOTES

1. *Engelhardt Report*, 1970, p. 30.

2. *Ibid.*, pp. 19-21.

3. See "Appendix C" for an analysis of the incidence of welfare.

EXHIBIT IV-41

CURRENT EXPENSE COST PER PUPIL * FOR SELECTED
NEW JERSEY MUNICIPALITIES

MUNICIPALITY	1964 to 1965	1965 to 1966	SCHOOL YEAR 1966 to 1967	1967 to 1968	1968 to 1969
Bayonne	$524	$543	$587	$645	$ 682
Bloomfield	585	612	659	705	757
Hackensack	721	759	772	862	1,032
Linden	593	635	655	714	820
Orange	551	632	701	735	775
Rahway	435	475	520	630	706
Scotch Plains	510	566	622	708	804
Westfield	527	560	606	641	754
Plainfield	523	577	641	720	782
Median	$527	$612	641	$708	$ 775
Interquartile range	$523-585	$560-632	$606-659	$645-735	$754-804

Source: N.J.E.A. Research Bulletin, "Basic Statistical Data of New Jersey School Districts."

*Total day school expenditures divided by total average daily enrollment; this is a current expense cost figure and does not include expenditures for debt service, budgeted capital outlay, or improvements authorizations.

EXHIBIT IV-42

TEACHERS' SALARIES PER PUPIL

MUNICIPALITY	1964 to 1965	1965 to 1966	SCHOOL YEAR 1966 to 1967	1967 to 1968	1968 to 1969
Bayonne	$308	$317	$346	$375	$412
Bloomfield	354	372	397	425	450
Hackensack	457	482	489	510	582
Linden	342	367	381	423	483
Orange	322	359	395	417	446
Rahway	283	309	327	370	441
Scotch Plains	301	319	353	388	436
Westfield	325	347	367	382	471
Plainfield	315	349	387	431	461
Median	322	349	381	417	450
Interquartile range	$308-342	$319-367	$353-395	$382-425	$441-471

Source: N.J.E.A. Research Bulletin, "Basic Statistical Data of New Jersey School Districts."

EXHIBIT IV-43

PROFESSIONAL STAFF MEMBERS PER 1,000 WEIGHTED PUPILS*

MUNICIPALITY	1964 to 1965	1965 to 1966	SCHOOL YEAR 1966 to 1967	1967 to 1968	1968 to 1969
Bayonne	47.3	47.5	47.5	50.2	51.4
Bloomfield	51.6	51.5	52.3	52.2	51.1
Hackensack	57.7	58.3	57.0	59.5	61.2
Linden	50.0	51.3	52.0	53.3	55.7
Orange	47.7	49.3	52.3	52.5	52.6
Rahway	44.8	46.9	48.8	51.8	53.4
Scotch Plains	47.5	49.1	51.0	52.0	51.7
Westfield	46.7	48.4	48.4	48.5	51.3
Plainfield	48.5	50.4	52.3	51.3	51.8
Median	47.7	49.3	52.0	52.0	51.8
Interquartile range	47.3-50.0	48.4-51.3	48.8-52.3	51.3-52.5	51.4-53.4

Source: N.J.E.A. Research Bulletin, "Basic Statistical Data of New Jersey School Districts."

*Total professional staff members (less nurses) divided by number of weighted** pupils in average daily enrollment in district schools expressed in thousands.

**By weighting enrollments, allowances are made for the difference in cost in providing kindergarten, elementary, secondary and special class programs. Weighting factors are: kindergarten — 0.5; elementary — 1.0; secondary — 1.3; special — 2.0.

Chapter V

ANALYSIS OF REVENUE SOURCES

The purpose of this chapter is to develop a broad overview of Plainfield's present revenue sources, show their patterns of change over the last five years and determine their potential growth.

The sources of revenue have been clustered based on the variables affecting them. The basic data source is the official financial statements of the city for the years 1965 through 1969. Exhibit V-1 displays the actual dollar value for each of the five clusters and their subgroups. Exhibit V-2 takes each year's total revenue by source and shows the percentage change.

RATIONALE FOR EACH CLUSTERED REVENUE SOURCE

Cluster No. 1. The first cluster consists of sources that are either based upon a previous year's tax levy or upon a service rendered by the city. This accounts for 8 percent of the total city revenue.

Sources for this cluster are: 1) surplus anticipated; 2) receipts from delinquent taxes; 3) sewer contracts; 4) parking authority contracts; 5) services in lieu of taxes.

The income from these sources has declined from over 13 percent of total revenues in 1965 to a little over 7 percent of revenues in 1969. However, the first two elements depend partly on previous years' tax levies, and changes in their level will reflect, at most, a change in one of the direct revenue sources. They therefore should not be used as an indicator of potential revenue sources.

The last three are presently independent of local control. Due to the

177

EXHIBIT V-1

TRENDS IN PLAINFIELD'S
REVENUE CATEGORIES

REVENUE CATEGORIES	YEAR				
	1965	1966	1967	1968	1969
Cluster No. 1					
Surplus	$ 1,100	$ 750	$ 565	$ 630	$ 585
Contract services	133	73	173	72	72
Services in lieu of taxes	67	62	58	61	60
Delinquent tax receipts	246	313	369	455	513
Cluster No. 2					
Miscellaneous collections	166	175	177	177	191
Interest on investments	166	171	249	310	439
Cluster No. 3					
Miscellaneous taxes	517	559	590	615	635
Cluster No. 4					
State aid (including replacement revenue)	189	181	219	861	1,047
Cluster No. 5					
Current property tax collections	8,278	8,649	10,117	11,159	12,051
Total	$10,862	$10,933	$12,517	$14,340	$15,593

Source: Financial Statements, City of Plainfield.
Note: Expenditure amounts are expressed in thousands of dollars.

EXHIBIT V-2

PERCENTAGE DISTRIBUTION OF EACH YEAR'S
REVENUE BY CATEGORY

REVENUE	YEAR				
	1965	1966	1967	1968	1969
Cluster No. 1					
Surplus	10.12%	6.86%	4.51%	4.39%	3.77%
Contract services	1.22	.66	1.38	.50	.46
Services in lieu of taxes	.61	.56	.46	.42	.39
Delinquent tax receipts	2.26	2.86	2.94	3.17	3.29
Cluster No. 2					
Miscellaneous collections	1.52	1.60	1.41	1.23	1.22
Interest on investments	1.52	1.56	1.98	2.16	2.81
Cluster No. 3					
Miscellaneous taxes	4.75	5.11	4.71	4.28	4.07
Cluster No. 4					
State aid (including replacement revenue)	1.74	1.61	1.74	6.00	6.71
Cluster No. 5					
Current property tax collections	76.21	79.14	80.82	77.81	77.28

Source: Financial Statements, City of Plainfield.

specificity of the former two and the absence of a cash flow for the latter, these three sources also should not be used as an indicator of potential revenue growth.

Cluster No. 2. The second cluster groups together miscellaneous collections made by various municipal departments: 1) licenses; 2) fees and permits; 3) fines; 4) interest on investments.

These sources have consistently remained at 4 percent of the total revenue. The major portion of the 4 percent consists of court fines, predominantly parking citations.

As an instrument to collect revenue, these sources must be viewed as undependable, placing a burden on the individual, thus creating an undesirable public image, and driving the cost of merchandise sold through licensed establishments to a level harmful to local merchants.

The fourth subgroup, interest on investments, accounts for the interest received from local banks during the time they hold city deposits. The dollar value is dependent upon both the volume of municipal deposits and the current interest rates.

Cluster No. 3. The third cluster consists of taxes that have statutory limitations placed upon them by state enabling acts. These include: 1) public utility franchise tax; 2) public utility gross receipts tax; 3) bus receipts tax.

While these miscellaneous taxes have increased slightly in size, as a share of total revenue they have slipped from 5 percent to 4 percent during the five-year tax period.

Since the bus receipts provide negligible revenue, only the first two will be considered here. The franchise tax (NJSA 54:30-1) applies to those corporations having equipment such as gas or electric lines on, under or around public property. It is administered and apportioned by the state at a fixed rate, and at set time intervals the funds are turned over to the municipalities.

The receipts tax (NJSA 54:30A-49) is similar in legal status and administration to the franchise tax; the state sets a rate of 8 percent on the gross receipts of public utility income collected within the municipality. In appraising their potential for increased future revenues, these sources must be considered independent of local control. If, however, they were to be increased, the increase would have to be passed on to the consumer, causing a higher burden on lower- and fixed-income citizens.

Cluster No. 4. The fourth cluster consists of the most important growth area in recent years. This includes the many different forms of state aid: aid to the municipal government; aid to the board of education; monies earmarked for specific projects; monies made available for uses determined by the city council; and a small amount of direct federal aid.

Exhibit V-3 lists the 13 revenue items provided by other governmental sources and shows a 66 percent increase in this source over the time period considered. This increase was necessitated by the state's removal of a large fraction of personal property from local tax rolls.

EXHIBIT V-3

STATUTORY USE CATEGORIES FOR
STATE AND FEDERAL AID COMING
INTO PLAINFIELD (1966 TO 1969)

AID CATEGORY	YEAR			
	1966	1967	1968	1969
State aid				
Road formula	$ 24	$ 23	$ 23	$ 23
Road construction		11	22	
Health		4	18	29
Library	18	20	31	34
Area library			44	54
Board of education	1,265	1,004	1,110	1,249
Community renewal	14	4		25
Model cities			7	111
Building aid schools	152	170	199	209
Uncommitted revenue to municipal government		11	599	779
Federal aid				
Library				
Community renewal	82	30		13
Model cities				34
Total	$1,555	$1,277	$2,053	$2,560

Source: Financial Statements, City of Plainfield.
Note: Monetary amounts are expressed in thousands of dollars.

The largest dollar value is aid to the board of education. This value, however, has not shown any rising trend. Rather, the most significant increase is in the category of uncommitted aid to municipal government.

Exhibit V-5 shows not only a minor growth in real estate value but also the value lost to the city from 1966 to 1967 because of the removal of the personal property tax base. The loss amounts to approximately $3,500,000. This reduction could involve close to $300,000 in revenue. This, however, is a paper figure. To offset this revenue loss, Chapter 135, Laws of 1966, as amended, contains a "save-harmless" provision whereby the municipalities will receive no less than the greater value of their personal property taxes for 1964, 1965, 1966 and 1967. This state replacement tax program has more than made up the estimated $300,000 loss of revenue in 1969 by a payment to the city of $588,000.

A second potentially expanding source of state aid comes from the state sales tax. At its 1968 rate of 3 percent, it generated $179,000 for the city. As of 1969, this rate had been increased to 5 percent. If the current apportionment formula is used and the inflationary period continues to increase state revenues by approximately 6 percent a year, then the city would be in line to receive $317,725 in the next fiscal year.

The remaining items in Exhibit V-3 are earmarked revenues; these show a consistent pattern for road repair and library aid. However, large sums of federal seed monies are arriving to aid planning and development of the poorer parts of the city.

Cluster No. 5. The fifth and last cluster, involving the property tax, is by far the most important revenue source for the city, providing 77 percent of the total revenues. During the past five years its revenues have increased from eight to $12 million, accounting for over 75 percent of total revenues each year. With present laws, this tax base is made up mostly of real property and a minor quantity of telephone and telegraph equipment.

To understand this source better and to estimate how much further it can be used, the real property base is subdivided into its components of residential, apartment house, commercial, industrial and vacant property. Exhibit V-4 shows the actual value of each of these classifications and the comparative stability of each unit from 1964 to 1969.

The combined residential, vacant and apartments columns for 1969 show that about 76 percent of this revenue source rests directly on homeowners or renters, 20 percent falls on commercial property, while 4 percent remains in industry.

EXHIBIT V-4

DOLLAR VALUE OF REAL ESTATE RATABLES BY TYPE OF PROPERTY

YEAR		RATABLE			
	Vacant Land	Residential Property (Excluding Apts.)	Commercial Property	Industrial Property	Apartments
1964	$1,911	$83,174	$24,968	$4,351	$10,902
1965	1,679	83,130	24,528	4,554	11,081
1966	1,917	83,055	24,904	4,486	11,733
1967	1,865	82,951	25,128	4,478	12,123
1968	2,054	82,832	25,671	4,227	11,789
1969	2,071	82,761	25,646	4,302	11,990

Source: Annual Reports, Office of the Tax Assessor, City of Plainfield.
Note: Monetary amounts are expressed in thousands of dollars.

In terms of growth the real property base has increased by less than 10 percent over the last five years. Can greater growth be anticipated?

The growth potential of the real property base can be viewed three different ways: 1) filling in the available vacant parcels with improvements; 2) demolishing existing improvements and replacing them with higher value improvements; 3) increasing the effective tax rate.

Exhibit V-5 shows that the number of vacant parcels has remained above the 550 level from 1964 to 1969. According to the community renewal program, they are widely distributed throughout the city, thus eliminating from consideration a comprehensive planned-unit development. Given their locations, the most probable use would be residential.

If these vacant parcels were to be brought into service, what value of tax revenue would they generate? This value can be estimated by projecting Plainfield's average value of a residential unit, $18,700, and assuming that equivalent ratables would be built on the vacant parcels.

Using the above procedure, property valued at $10.6 million would be constructed. Using the effective tax rate of 5.4 percent, only 375,000 in new taxes would be generated. This hypothetical revenue might not even cover the increased costs for education, police, fire, etc.

Other ways of filling the vacant property would include some combination of residential, commercial and industrial development. The lack of growth in the commercial and industrial base, together with the dispersed nature of the parcels, raises questions about the practicality of securing such development on a significant scale.

The second alternative for suggesting growth in the tax base is to analyze the pattern of improvements over the last five years. The basic data are shown in Exhibit V-6. On the average, $290,000 worth of property improvements have been demolished each year, being replaced on the average with $1,334,000 worth of new improvements. At the 1970 effective tax rate of 5 percent, this allowed a net increase in average valuation of $1,044,000 and generated approximately $50,000 in taxes in the current year.

The last alternative is an increase in the effective tax rate. Exhibit V-7 shows the level to which this mechanism has been utilized. Exhibit V-8 indicates that from 1968 to 1969 the total taxable value of property increased by about $400,000, while Exhibit V-1 shows a $900,000 increase in property tax revenue.

EXHIBIT V-5 (I)

NUMBER OF REAL ESTATE ITEMS BY CLASS

YEAR	Vacant Parcels	ITEM				
		1-Family	2-Family	3-Family	4-Family	5-to-9-Family
1964	623	6,889	1,546	223	148	75
1965	584	6,770	1,700	265	150	66
1966	585	6,735	1,680	259	145	62
1967	559	6,741	1,649	255	140	65
1968	589	6,737	1,631	253	140	64
1969	571	6,733	1,624	265	144	66

Source: Annual Reports, Office of the Tax Assessor, City of Plainfield.

EXHIBIT V-5 (II)

NUMBER OF REAL ESTATE ITEMS BY CLASS

YEAR	Apartment Buildings No. of Buildings	No. of Units	Dwellings in Commercial Buildings	ITEM Garden Apartments No. of Buildings	No. of Units	Commercial Buildings	Industrial Buildings
1964	34	934	—	16	1,161	815	47
1965	44	1,174	863	16	1,424	789	51
1966	39	1,114	1,023	14	1,176	789	54
1967	42	1,262	1,008	13	1,109	787	54
1968	45	1,397	939	14	1,176	786	51
1969	45	1,346	895	14	1,145	784	52

Source: Annual Reports, Office of the Tax Assessor, City of Plainfield.

EXHIBIT V-6

MONETARY VALUE OF IMPROVEMENTS

YEAR	Taxable Value of Improvements Demolished	Improved This Year Exempt from Taxation	Taxable Value New Construction	Improved Last Year Taxable This Year	Total Increase Improvement Ratables
1964	$194	$ 644	$1,308	$25	$495
1965	384	1,001	1,409	7	31
1966	480	287	1,447	9	697
1967	402	621	1,375	5	356
1968	180	1,402	1,534	8	41
1969	96	620	933	10	227

Source: Annual Reports, Office of the Tax Assessor, City of Plainfield.

Note: Monetary amounts are expressed in thousands of dollars.

Since the increased valuation brought only $20,000 in new revenue, the balance was made up by the increased tax rate. From 1964 to 1970 the effective tax rate went from $3.35 to $5.40. The question becomes how high this rate can go without injuring the citizens it is meant to serve.

Exhibit V-9 shows that in 1970 Plainfield had the highest effective tax rate in the county. Comparison of this level of tax rate with that of the other municipalities in New Jersey shows that Plainfield is presently in the highest tax rate grouping in the state.

DEGENERATION OF REALTY TAX COLLECTIONS

Exhibit V-10 indicates that, over the three periods analyzed, Plainfield's comparative tax rate position has maintained its high relative ranking to the point that further tax-rate increases may not be possible.

Within the property tax base, uncollected taxes and assessment reductions work to decrease revenues. Exhibit V-11 illustrates the increasing problem of uncollected taxes. Over the five-year period this yearly loss has increased by several hundred thousand dollars. Within this loss is the second factor, assessment reductions by the county courts. Exhibit V-12 reveals the uneven pattern of actual tax dollars lost and the corresponding reductions from the tax base of an annual average of $911,000 worth of property. The capitalization of the real estate tax has begun to erode significantly the market value and assess-

EXHIBIT V-7

ESTIMATED EFFECTIVE PROPERTY TAX RATE FOR
PLAINFIELD BY YEAR IN DOLLARS TAXED FOR
$100 OF REAL PROPERTY

YEAR	Effective (True) Tax Rate	General Tax Rate	Equalization Ratio x 100	Percentage Change in the Equalization Ratio
1964	$3.35	$10.58	$31.71	
1965	3.65	6.60	55.31	
1966	3.63	6.90	52.66	4.8%
1967	3.97	8.04	49.39	6.2
1968	4.43	9.11	48.62	1.6
1969	4.64	9.81	47.27	2.8
1970	5.40	11.52	46.89	.8

Source: Financial Reports, City of Plainfield.
Note: Effective Tax Rate = General Tax Rate x County Equalization Ratio.
County Equalization Ratio is the ratio of the actual assessed value of the aggregate
real property of Plainfield to the independently estimated tax value of that property.

EXHIBIT V-8

ASSESSED DOLLAR VALUE OF TAXABLE PROPERTY IN PLAINFIELD

YEAR	Taxable Value of Land	Taxable Value of Improvements	Total Taxable Value of Real Estate	Total Taxable Value of Personal Property	Total Taxable Value of Real and Personal Property
1964	$37,905	$87,403	$125,532	$8,074	$133,623
1965	37,565	87,434	125,237	7,536	132,773
1966	37,992	88,132	126,124	7,790	133,914
1967	38,080	88,488	126,569	4,134*	130,703
1968	38,148	88,447	126,595	4,111	130,706
1969	38,132	88,647	126,779	4,351	131,130

Source: Annual Reports, Office of the Tax Assessor, City of Plainfield.

Note: Monetary amounts are expressed in thousands of dollars.

*Decrease due to elimination of all tangible business personal property from the city's assessment roll.

EXHIBIT V-9

EFFECTIVE TAX RATES FOR THE MUNICIPALITIES IN UNION COUNTY, NEW JERSEY

Municipalities (UNION COUNTY)	EFFECTIVE TAX RATE (1970)
Berkeley Heights	$2.22
Clark	3.21
Cranford	3.40
Elizabeth	4.17
Fanwood	4.19
Garwood	3.11
Hillside	3.31
Kenilworth	2.44
Linden	2.20
Mountainside	3.03
New Providence	2.45
Plainfield	5.40
Rahway	3.58
Roselle	3.32
Roselle Park	3.75
Scotch Plains	3.84
Springfield	3.44
Summit	2.94
Union	2.49
Westfield	3.44
Winfield	2.12

Source: County of Union, Tax Rate Report.

EXHIBIT V-10

COMPARISON OF MUNICIPAL EFFECTIVE TAX RATE GROWTH: 1960, 1965 AND 1969 FOR ALL 566 NEW JERSEY MUNICIPALITIES

TAX RATE GROUP	YEAR 1960		YEAR 1965		YEAR 1969	
	No.	%	No.	%	No.	%
Under $1.00	8	1.4%	7	1.2%	6	1.0%
$1.00 to $1.99	156	27.5	78	13.8	29	5.1
$2.00 to $2.99	336	59.3	311	54.9	147	25.9
$3.00 to $3.99	52	9.2	151	26.6	277	48.9
Over $4.00	15	2.6	20	3.5	108	19.1
Plainfield effective tax rate	$3.07		$3.65		$4.64	

Source: Mimeographed Report, New Jersey Division of Taxation.

EXHIBIT V-11

COMPARISON OF TAX LEVIES AND COLLECTIONS
AS OF DECEMBER 31, 1969

YEAR	Tax Levy	Cash Collection	Difference Between Levy & Current Collections	Percentage Collected
1965	$ 8,681	$ 8,278	$403	95.3%
1966	9,031	8,650	381	95.8
1967	10,635	10,117	518	95.1
1968	11,792	11,159	633	94.6
1969	12,715	12,051	664	94.8

Source: Financial Reports, City of Plainfiela.
Note: Monetary amounts are expressed in thousands of dollars.

EXHIBIT V-12

TAX WRITE-OFFS FOR PLAINFIELD
BY THE COUNTY COURTS

YEAR	Value of Tax Reduction	Value of Property Lost From Tax Base
1964	$22	$ 657
1965	66	1,808
1966	4	110
1967	34	856
1968	69	1,558
1969	22	474

Source: Financial Reports, City of Plainfield.
Note: Monetary amounts are expressed in thousands of dollars.

ment base of real property. In Newark the real estate tax collection ratio has fallen to 87 percent. Must Plainfield follow?[1]

* * *

The Plainfield revenue structure is composed of a set of sources that are: capable of only slight change but which are insignificant in revenue power; set at a state statutory limit and, therefore, out of the legislative control of the city council; and anchored by a high yield property tax that is one of the highest in the state and not capable of significant expansion without self-destructive repercussions.

SUMMARY

Plainfield receives its revenue dollars from many sources, both inside and outside its boundaries. To evaluate the performance of these sources, five clusters were constructed from the individual source elements; each cluster contains elements similar in legal constraints and revenue potential.

Cluster No. 1 contains revenue elements whose money value depends on previous commitments such as delinquent tax receipts or the surplus reserved for the present year's uncollected taxes. Its percentage of the total revenue has declined from 14 percent in 1965 to 8 percent in 1969. Being composed of previous commitments, this cluster should not be thought of as a source of new revenue.

Cluster No. 2 contains miscellaneous revenue elements such as interest on investments and traffic violation tickets. Its percentage of the total revenue has increased from 3 percent in 1965 to 4 percent in 1969. The very limited base for this revenue cluster will not allow it to expand at much over the inflationary rate.

Cluster No. 3 contains miscellaneous taxes excluding the property tax. Their rates are set by state statute and allowed collection of 5 percent of the total revenue in 1965, but declined to 4 percent in 1969. Revenue potential is limited both by state statute and their regressive impact.

Cluster No. 4 contains extragovernmental grants mostly from the state. This cluster has increased in importance from 2 percent to 7 percent and, from the viewpoint of Plainfield, offers the only tolerable source of new revenue.

Cluster No. 5 contains the only remaining source—the property tax. It has accounted consistently for over 76 percent of the revenue gained by the city during a period when the total revenue required to provide governmental services has increased from $11 million (in 1965) to $16 million (in 1969). Its potential for future revenue increases is limited by the negligible potential for an increase in the property tax base and the present 5 percent effective tax rate which is reducing the market value of the taxable property.

The conclusion is clear. The revenue structure composed of the five clusters is essentially inflexible when viewed from the standpoint of Plainfield's legal authority. Any change in Cluster No. 1, No. 2, No. 3 or No. 5 will provoke self-defeating consequences upon the city. Extragovernmental grants, included in Cluster No. 4, present the only viable alternatives for the city.

EXHIBIT V-13

PROJECTED REVENUES FOR PLAINFIELD FOR 1970 TO 1975,
ASSUMING THE CONTINUING REAL TAX RATE OF $11.52

REVENUE CATEGORY	Actual Revenue 1969	Average Percent Change	1970	1971	1972	1973	1974	1975
Cluster No. 1	$ 1,230	2.7%	$ 1,263	$ 1,297	$ 1,332	$ 1,368	$ 1,405	$ 1,443
Cluster No. 2	191	3.8	198	206	214	222	230	239
Cluster No. 3	635	5.7	671	709	749	792	837	885
Cluster No. 4	2,560	—*	2,878	3,065	3,264	3,476	3,702	3,943
Cluster No. 5	12,051	—*	14,275	14,341	14,375	14,408	14,442	14,475
Total projected revenue	$16,667		$19,285	$19,618	$19,934	$20,266	$20,616	$20,985

Source: Plainfield Study, 1970.

Note: Monetary amounts are expressed in thousands of dollars.

*Incrementing methods are described in text, Chapter V, p. 188.

REVENUE AND EXPENDITURE PROJECTIONS
THROUGH 1975

Plainfield's future service delivery system is largely dependent on its own resources. Can local resources meet the challenge? Plainly, the answer is negative.

One of the major goals of this chapter, as stated previously, is to determine the dollar gap resulting from continuing present expenditure patterns for public services on an increasingly insufficient fixed revenue base.

Revenue sources were projected by using the 1969 revenue values for the five clusters of revenue sources as bases and calculating probable changes for 1970 to 1975. The clusters were defined earlier in this chapter.

REVENUE PROJECTION

The yearly increments for Clusters No. 1, No. 2 and No. 3 are calculated by multiplying the previous year's value by the average percentage change from 1965 to 1969. The results of this process are displayed in Exhibit V-13.

The results from Cluster No. 1 should be interpreted cautiously, for it must be remembered that these revenues are conjectural, based upon commitments and difficulties faced by citizens in paying their previous tax bills. Most of the increase over the last three years has resulted from larger payments of delinquent taxes, probably because payment is easier with present inflated wages than with wages at the time the tax bill was levied. Nonetheless, the conditions of inflated prices and advancing unemployment may make any further increase in this sector questionable. The projections of Clusters No. 2 and No. 3 do not suffer from similar problems.

Cluster No. 4 depends basically on grants-in-aid and uncommitted funds from the state government. From 1968 to 1969, the last two years of available complete data, a sharp rise in federal funds through the community renewal and model cities programs probably overstated the possibilities for extra federal support in the future. Federal funds are meant to be seed monies for programs to be picked up by local government eventually. The projection would thus be overly optimistic if it were to allow the sharp rise in federal funds as shown in Cluster No. 4 to govern the calculations totally. In essence, the increases here may be viewed as step increments rather than the product of increased trends.

The one increase that may be considered probable is the change in the sales tax rate. The 3 percent rate of 1968 produced a payment to the city of 179,290. If this base is then subjected to an estimated increase of

4.8 percent for inflation plus 1.7 percent for growth in population, then the new 5 percent rate should allow for a payment of $316,233.[2] The last revenue source is the property tax listed as Cluster No. 5. The property tax, unlike the preceding four groups, has two variable elements that can be changed for the purpose of projecting future revenue: first, the total assessed value of taxable property; and second, the property tax rate. Throughout this analysis, except where designated otherwise, the continuation of the 1970 general tax rate of $11.52 is assumed, which, when recalculated to reflect the effective tax rate, is $5.42.

Thus, with the tax rate held constant, only the projected increase in the valuation of taxable property will affect the revenue gained by Cluster No. 5. Four steps are required for the calculation of the projected revenue: 1) start with the preceding year's total assessed property tax base as shown in Exhibit V-8; 2) add the average yearly increase in improvement derived from Exhibit V-9 ($375,000); 3) calculate the tax levy by using the general tax rate (11.52 percent); 4) calculate actual collections by assuming only 94.5 percent of the levy collected.[3] The result of these calculations is also shown in Exhibit V-17: it shows a continuous but slow rise in tax revenue as long as we assume that the tax rate is maintained at its present level. The question is, then, will these projected revenues be sufficient to meet future needs? Discussion of this question follows.

EXPENDITURE PROJECTIONS

Chapter II presented the existing information regarding expenditure patterns in the past. This must be projected into the 1975 calendar and school year.

MUNICIPAL PROJECTIONS

Chapter III provided an in-depth analysis of projected needs for the most important municipal functions. Exhibit V-14 summarizes these findings.

BOARD OF EDUCATION EXPENDITURES

The board of education analysis has proceeded somewhat differently. In Chapter IV the various programs within the school system were described. However, because of the lack of important expenditure data, the level of future needs in terms of new services and programs in education is far from definitive.

Each expenditure category has been described in Chapter IV; now, based upon the average percentage change for each of these categories over the previous five years, the yearly expenditure for education is

EXHIBIT V-14

SUMMARY OF ALL PROJECTED EXPENDITURES
FOR MUNICIPAL AND BOARD OF EDUCATION ITEMS

ITEM	Appropriation 1970	YEAR				
		1971	1972	1973	1974	1975
General government	$ 530	$ 599	$ 679	$ 770	$ 874	$ 994
Administration & finance	304	320	336	353	370	388
Public works	1,060	1,113	1,169	1,227	1,288	1,352
Miscellaneous*	3,251	3,575	3,960	4,411	4,944	5,583
Police	1,764	1,961	2,179	2,423	2,693	2,995
Fire	1,511	1,674	1,855	2,057	2,282	2,531
Welfare	173	181	190	199	208	217
Library	382	405	432	461	492	525
Health	232	244	256	268	284	298
Recreation	219	231	246	261	279	299
Education	9,810	10,688	11,646	13,079	13,845	15,110
Total projected expenditures and projected revenue needs	$19,236	$20,991	$22,948	$25,509	$27,559	$30,292
Total projected revenue	$19,285	$19,618	$19,934	$20,266	$20,616	$20,985
Dollar gap		$ 1,373	$ 3,014	$ 5,243	$ 6,943	$ 9,307

Source: Municipal government data; Board of education data; Plainfield Study, 1970.
Note: Monetary amounts are expressed in thousands of dollars.
*This value has been derived by subtracting the library expenditure from the total projected expenditures row of Exhibit III-47.

projected through the 1975-1976 school year. This is shown in Exhibit V-15.

Are these projections appropriate? How much are they affected by unique situations occurring during the previous period?

Three events or trends can be viewed as having affected expenditures significantly during the past five years: 1) the progressive increase of inflation as indicated by the Consumer Price Index; 2) the civil unrest breaking out in 1967; and 3) the recent completion and operation of the new high school.

Inflation. The average yearly percent change value used for each category has imbedded within it the inflationary trend and its assumed continuance. This is perhaps understated; the value is an average for

EXHIBIT V-15

PROJECTED EXPENDITURES FOR THE PLAINFIELD BOARD OF
EDUCATION FROM 1971-72 TO 1975-76

EXPENDITURE ITEM	Average Yearly Percent Change	1970 to 1971 Appropriation	1971 to 1972	1972 to 1973	1973 to 1974	1974 to 1975	1975 to 1976
Personnel							
Administration	6.9%	$ 313	$ 335	$ 358	$ 383	$ 409	$ 437
Teachers	8.2	5,098	5,516	5,968	6,457	6,986	7,559
Principals	8.8	427	465	506	551	599	652
Supervisors	10.2	174	192	212	234	258	284
Other instructional personnel	8.8	552	601	654	712	775	843
Clerical	6.9	231	247	264	282	301	322
Operations	7.3	739	793	851	913	980	1,052
Maintenance	8.8	110	120	131	143	156	170
Administration							
Contractual services	8.8	29	32	35	38	41	45
Other	16.4	42	49	57	66	77	90
Instruction							
Textbooks	11.4	88	98	109	121	135	150
Library & A-V	14.9	59	68	78	90	103	118
Teaching supplies	4.5	119	124	130	136	142	148
Other	9.9	134	147	162	178	196	215

EXHIBIT V-15 (Continued)

PROJECTED EXPENDITURES FOR THE PLAINFIELD BOARD OF
EDUCATION FROM 1971-72 TO 1975-76

EXPENDITURE ITEM	Average Yearly Percent Change	1970 to 1971 Appropriation	1971 to 1972	1972 to 1973	1973 to 1974	1974 to 1975	1975 to 1976
Operations							
Heat	9.9%	$ 68	$ 75	$ 82	$ 90	$ 99	$ 109
Utilities	6.0	125	133	141	149	153	167
Supplies	6.8	25	27	29	31	33	35
Other	4.8	11	12	13	14	15	16
Fixed charges							
Pensions	12.0	152	170	190	213	239	268
Insurance	11.0	280	311	345	383	425	472
Tuition	8.5	66	72	78	85	92	100
Maintenance							
Contractual services	10.6	117	129	143	158	175	198
Equipment replacement	18.7	45	53	63	75	89	106
Other	7.0	57	61	65	70	75	80
Minor expenditure category	14.5	749	858	982	1,124	1,287	1,474
Total		$9,810	$10,688	$11,646	$12,696	$13,845	$15,110

Source: Budget Statement, Board of Education.
Note: Monetary amounts are expressed in thousands of dollars.

five years, while the current rate is higher.

Civil Unrest. Civil disturbances can be said to have had a direct influence on three categories: number of operating personnel; increased turnover in administration, causing increased operating costs; and lastly, increases in insurance.

Conservative approaches have been used in viewing the future of these expenditures. The assumption has been made that the insurance rates and the security force will remain at their present level while the rate of increase in services contracted from outside the school system will decline to the average level of change existing from 1965 to 1967.

High School. Finally, in the absence of informed opinion by the high school administration, it must be assumed that the maintenance, operation and program development will proceed at the same rate as in the past.

Projection Rationale for Board of Education

Salaries. Wages and salaries for district personnel account for the greatest dollar increase. Exhibit V-16 shows that these salary increases are common to New Jersey school districts. In each case the projection rate used in this study is below the most recent change rate. It was found from the analysis in Chapter II that Plainfield is maintaining only average salary levels; thus, to maintain the professional level one would expect that the city would attempt to remain within the mainstream of regional salaries rather than depend on teaching staff subsidization of education through relatively low salaries.

Staff Size. The second increase results from additional employees. It is assumed, however, that the present staff level will remain constant. (However, the potential exists for an increase in the student body as a result of changing demographic trends earlier indicated in this study.)

EXHIBIT V-16

MEDIAN TEACHERS' SALARIES COST PER PUPIL
FOR NEW JERSEY SCHOOL DISTRICTS

YEAR	Median Salary	Percentage Change
1964 to 1965	$293	
1965 to 1966	313	6.8%
1966 to 1967	338	7.9
1967 to 1968	366	8.2
1968 to 1969	405	10.7

Source: NJEA Research Bulletin, "Basic Statistics for New Jersey School Districts."

The rate of change in salary expenditures has therefore been projected by determining the rate of increase for the average salary or wage for each personnel category. This change rate is then applied to the existing staff expenditure levels.

This methodology must be viewed as conservative. The trend in education is to further individualization of instruction. (Exhibit IV-41 shows the number of teachers per 1000 weighted pupils.) About 50 percent of northern New Jersey districts examined have a higher ratio of teachers to pupils than Plainfield; given the local interest in education, it is reasonable to assume that there will be a tendency to improve this ratio.

Finally, what may happen if the inflationary trend declines? Will expenditures decrease at a similar rate? Unfortunately this is a substantial question. Costs subsumed under labor have been generally recognized as being sticky in their decline; it is much more difficult to lower wages than to raise them. Since 89 percent of the budget goes for some kind of labor service, no substantial relief can be expected under this condition.

* * *

Therefore it must be concluded that the 55 percent increase in the size of the board of education budget as measured from 1970-1971 to the 1975-1976 school year is consistent with a reasonable interpretation of present cost trends. This estimate may prove to be conservative depending on the increased militancy of municipal employee unions, potential shifts in the student body and basic inflationary increments.

THE DOLLAR GAP

Through the various sections of this report, the different public services provided by municipal and board of education departments have been analyzed. Exhibit V-14 summarizes the expenditure needs for both of these governmental units and projected revenues. The dollar gap in 1971 is $1,393,000; in 1972 it is $3,073,000; in 1973 it is $5,269,000; in 1974 it is $6,928,000; and in 1975 it is $9,249,000.

For each year the expenditures exceed the revenues. What mechanism can be used to balance these figures? The only significant instrument currently within the hands of local government is the property tax rate; thus, the property tax rate will have to be increased if there is to be a balanced budget. Exhibit V-17 shows the results.

Unless substantial alternative revenue sources are made available, Plainfield's effective tax rate will increase to $8.38 per $100 of true property value.

EXHIBIT V-17

PROJECTED TAX RATES

	YEAR					
	1970	1971	1972	1973	1974	1975
(1) Projected revenue needs	$ 19,186	$ 20,976	$ 22,935	$ 25,496	$ 27,544	$ 30,279
(2) Revenues exclusive of property tax	5,027	5,010	5,277	5,858	6,174	6,510
(3) Property tax needed to be collected	14,159	15,966	17,658	19,638	21,370	23,769
(4) Projected tax base	131,505	131,880	132,255	132,630	133,005	133,380
(5) General tax rate needed to collect projected property tax	11.39	12.80	14.20	15.62	17.00	18.90
(6) Equalization ratio	46.89	46.42	45.96	45.50	45.04	44.59
(7) Effective tax rate	5.34	5.94	6.50	7.11	7.70	8.38

Sources: For line (1) see Exhibit V-14; for line (2) see Exhibit V-13, "total projected revenue," Cluster No. 5; for line (3) see lines (1) and (2); for line (4) see Exhibit V-8, p. 186; for line (5) see formula below; for line (6) see Exhibit V-7, p. 185; for line (7) see formula below; for line (8) $375,000 — see p. 192 of text; for line (9) 94.5% — see p. 192 of text.

Formulas Used to Calculate the Property Tax Rates

$$\text{General tax rate on real and personal property} = \frac{\left[\text{property tax needed to be collected}\right]}{\left[\text{preceding year's real and personal tax base} + \text{estimated value of new improvements}\right]\left[\text{collection rate}\right]}$$

$$(5) = \frac{(3)}{[(4) + (\$375,000)]\,[94.5\%^{a}]}$$

$$\text{true tax rate} = \left[\text{real tax rate on real and personal property}\right]\left[\text{equalization ratio}\right]$$

$$(7) = [5]\,[6]$$

*Numbers in parentheses refer to sources above.

a. See p. 192.

Plainfield will have joined the ranks of the Newarks and the Hobokens and the older core cities where home ownership is the shortest path to fiscal disaster. This is of significance to more than just Plainfield homeowners. The functions of the older suburb within our society are complex, but certainly one of prime importance is its service as a rung in the ladder of upward mobility for emerging ghetto dwellers. Unless there is a very complete re-evaluation of how their services are financed, the older suburbs will no longer be able to serve this function. The zone of emergence will become a *zone of despair*—the line of upward mobility will abort. And Plainfield is not alone.

FOOTNOTES

1. The decline in tax collection ratios in areas of high tax rates is assuming ominous proportions nationally. See George Sternlieb, *Some Aspects of the Abandoned House Problem*, Rutgers, 1970.

2. The 1.7 percent addendum is overly optimistic, given the growth of general population within the state and present allocation methods.

3. The assumption that only 94.5 percent of the property tax levy will be actually collected reflects both the trend of tax write-offs through county judgements and nonpayment of the tax by property owners. The value used is a conservative figure based upon the 1969 collection rate; estimates by the department of finance suggest the possibility of a 91 percent collection rate and the probability of even lower collection levels if the tax rate is increased.

Appendix A

TELEPHONE SURVEY METHODOLOGY

The telephone survey was based on the April 1970 Plainfield telephone directory. There are 331 pages in this directory. The first and the last Plainfield listing on each page was chosen, yielding 662 numbers. The disposition of these listings follows:

Completed	441
Moved	46*
Refusals	67
Disconnects	37
No answer after four or more calls	71
Total	662

*These families maintained their former Plainfield telephone listing

COMPARABILITY OF THE TELEPHONE SAMPLE TO THE HOUSING DISTRIBUTION OF THE CITY

Based on information from the assessor's office, one-family houses make up 60 percent of the city's housing units. For the telephone respondents, the equivalent was 60 percent. Two-family houses make up 14 percent of the total housing units but only 13 percent for the telephone sample. Three- and four-family houses, according to the assessor's office, provided 4 percent of the city's residential units. The equivalent figure for the sample was 5 percent. Structures with five or more apartments made up 23 percent of the city's housing stock. In the sample the equivalent figure was 23 percent.

It should be noted, however, that the sampling technique tends to exclude rooming houses for boarders as well as institutional facilities. In addition, there is a skew resulting from the no answer and refusal category. Subject to this, however, the basic consistency between the telephone survey respondents' housing and the city's as a whole seems clear.

However, the limitations of such a methodology, in terms of demographic extrapolation, are evident. By the nature of its structure, it tends to underrepresent those segments of the population which do not have telephones. In the case of Plainfield, 94 percent of households have telephones. Unfortunately, not all of these are listed and there are no adequate data on the socioeconomic characteristics of the holders of unlisted telephone numbers. Based on a previous survey conducted elsewhere by the research team, holders of unlisted numbers were, surprisingly enough, noted across socioeconomic lines. Nonrespondents are a more significant problem. Small households with no children or those with all family members working are underrepresented.

To forestall this difficulty, as many as six callbacks were conducted. Despite this effort, only 441 of the previously chosen listings were successfully completed. The findings, therefore, are to be viewed more as indications of variation in attitude than definitive of themselves. Unfortunately, at this writing the 1970 census results are not available. There is some indication, however, that the number of minority group residents within the city is understated. While this precludes demographic mix for the entire city, it does not inhibit insight into variations in the attitudes of minority-group members as contrasted with equivalent groups of whites within the community.

OWNERS VERSUS RENTERS

In 1960, 55 percent of the homes in Plainfield were owned by their residents. In the telephone survey the equivalent figure is 59 percent. Given the rough equivalents of building ratios in the 10 years since 1960, there is some indication that owners are slightly overrepresented in the sample in contrast to renters. However, examining the owners and the renters as separate units provides insights into their characteristics and desires.

The telephone technique, therefore, makes sweeping projections more subject to error than generalizations based on the subsets and their cross-tabulation.

NEW HOME BUYERS: SAMPLING TECHNIQUE

1) All property transfers for 1969 in the City of Plainfield were counted. Transfers excluded (which totalled a 10 percent rejection) were: 1) all nominal transfers; e.g., "$1.00 consideration," "$100 or under," and "$50 or under"; "no consideration"; 2) Those transfers going to buyers who were known realtors; 3) Commercial transfers; 4) Civil actions.

2) There were 841 transfers.

Ward #	No.
1	118
2	316
3	163
4	244

3) In order to obtain 100 samples, every eighth transfer was picked ($841/100 = 8.4$).

4) Selection started from the first transfer in the third ward (selected randomly) and continued through all four wards until all four ward books were exhausted. This resulted in a total of 107 selections.

5) If one of the selected samples was a member of an excluded category, the next transfer in the book was used.

6) Out of the 107 selected transfers, 71 respondents were interviewed. The level of success follows:

Completed	51
Not at home	11
Refusals	5
Vacant	3
Commercial	1
Total	71

Appendix C

THE WELFARE BURDEN

In 1965 Plainfield had 1,326 people on welfare. In 1970, there were 3,741 welfare recipients. Behind these numbers lies the reality—nearly 9 percent of the city's population must receive public support. And welfare payments per se are an inadequate measure of the municipality's total cost in supplying the needs of the poor. Both in terms of increased education, police and health department expenditures and augmented municipal staff needed to coordinate federal programs, the poor cost more. While Chapter III concentrated on direct municipal welfare charges, this appendix investigates an aspect of the pattern, i.e., the change in the number of welfare cases occurring in Plainfield and the other municipalities of Union County as administered by the Union County Welfare Department over the years 1965 to 1970.

The specific reasons for the increased welfare load are for the most part unavailable for public review. Union County administers 96 percent of the welfare payments to Plainfield residents, the remaining 4 percent being served through municipal public assistance; however, information indicating whether the persons involved are immigrants, local citizens unable to meet their budget or persons temporarily unemployed, is not available. Thus, the yearly change in caseload by welfare category for Plainfield and a comparison with the other municipalities within Union County are all that can be furnished.

ANALYSIS OF UNION COUNTY WELFARE CASELOAD
AS APPLICABLE TO PLAINFIELD

Welfare payments are for the most part distributed through four programs: 1) assistance for dependent children (ADC); 2) disability assistance; 3) old age assistance; and 4) assistance for the blind.[1]

Exhibits C-1 and C-2 show the patterns of ADC caseloads and total public assistance in the municipalities within Union County for the years 1965 to 1970.

CONSEQUENCES OF THE HIGH WELFARE LOAD

What does it mean for a city to have nearly 9 percent of its population living on welfare? Consider alone that element with the largest im-

EXHIBIT C-1

AVERAGE MONTHLY NUMBER OF ADC
RECIPIENTS IN EACH UNION COUNTY
MUNICIPALITY
(1965 TO 1970)

MUNICIPALITY	YEAR					
	1965[a]	1966[b]	1967[c]	1968[d]	1969[e]	1970 (August)[f]
Berkeley Heights	2	0	4	3	5	2
Clark	13	4	4	11	22	48
Cranford	44	36	46	58	114	138
Elizabeth	2,500	2,400	3,040	3,532	5,581	6,871
Fanwood	9	8	4	12	17	41
Garwood	14	4	4	11	34	52
Hillside	14	16	6	61	115	209
Kenilworth	22	20	6	13	47	71
Linden	255	252	290	499	717	1,171
Mountainside	0	0	0	4	0	0
New Providence	1	4	4	13	11	21
Plainfield	1,100	1,000	1,220	1,558	2,590	3,516
Rahway	154	116	152	179	367	610
Roselle	242	204	276	251	566	731
Roselle Park	31	28	46	48	57	123
Scotch Plains	26	28	30	44	65	95
Springfield	14	8	30	31	36	71
Summit	62	52	57	54	99	125
Union	148	132	140	186	324	468
Westfield	36	24	57	50	58	112
Winfield		4	4	5	17	25
Out of county	31	36	38	91	107	117
Out of state	2		0			3
Total	4,720	4,732	5,458	6,714	10,949	14,620

Source: Annual Report, Union County Welfare Board.
[a]Number of persons calculated from the average family size per case was 4.4 in 1965.
[b]Number of persons calculated from an assumed average family size per case of 4.0.
[c]Number of persons calculated from the average family size per case was 3.8 in 1967.
[d]Number of persons on active case load for month of December.
[e]Number of persons on active case load for month of October.
[f]Number of persons on active case load for month of August.

pact on municipal services—the children. Based on the ADC record, more than 2,500 children live under conditions of welfare. This means that as many as one out of five children in Plainfield's public schools may be on welfare.

Plainfield and several of the other older cities listed in Exhibit C-1 are subsidizing the many other communities within the county which have been able to avoid the problem practically completely.

A further analysis reveals the extent of this subsidy by determining the number of persons on county welfare for every 1,000 persons living in each municipality within the county. Exhibit C-2 displays these data and the calculated ratio of welfare cases to population of the municipalities. Plainfield's index of 73 welfare persons for every 1,000 population is by far the highest in Union county.

EXHIBIT C-2

NUMBER OF WELFARE RECIPIENTS
PER 1,000 RESIDENTS OF EACH
MUNICIPALITY IN UNION COUNTY

MUNICIPALITY	(1) Estimated 1969 Population	(2) Total Number of Union County Welfare Supported Persons as of August 1970	Welfare Persons Per 1,000 Population
Berkeley Heights	12,710	14	1.1
Clark	19,410	50	2.6
Cranford	29,070	151	5.2
Elizabeth	119,170	7,547	63.3
Fanwood	9,360	47	5.0
Garwood	6,050	55	9.1
Hillside	23,620	231	9.8
Kenilworth	9,420	79	8.4
Linden	45,670	1,280	28.0
Mountainside	8,120	1	.1
New Providence	14,050	22	1.6
Plainfield	50,590	3,741	73.9
Rahway	31,560	672	21.2
Roselle	24,300	787	32.4
Roselle Park	15,650	130	8.3
Scotch Plains	24,330	109	4.5
Springfield	16,580	82	4.9
Summit	25,210	165	6.5
Union	57,310	523	9.1
Westfield	34,670	135	3.9
Winfield	2,530	25	9.9

Sources: Column (1) is from New Jersey Economic Review, Vol. XI, No. 6, 1969, pp. 14-20. Column (2) is derived from the sum of the ADC, old age and disability categories of assistance.

FOOTNOTES

1. For a family to take advantage of the ADC category it must reside in New Jersey and have dependent children who have been deprived of support or care by reason of death, physical or mental incapacity, insufficient earnings, unemployment or continued absence from the home of one or both of the natural or adoptive parents.

   Disability assistance offers support to persons ages 18 through 64 who are permanently and totally disabled by either physical or mental defects.

   Old age assistance grants support payments to those persons 65 years old and over who are without either support or responsible relatives willing or able to support them.

   The last category, assistance for the blind, supports legally blind adults who have no other means of maintaining themselves.